'Working collaboratively is a vital p
This book is comprehensive, prac
tips and insights on the subject. I'
ful resource to churches and othe̶ ̶C̶h̶r̶i̶s̶t̶i̶a̶n̶ ̶o̶r̶g̶a̶n̶i̶z̶a̶t̶i̶o̶n̶s̶ ̶a̶s̶ ̶t̶h̶e̶y̶
continue to seek a Christ-inspired, unified approach to ministry.'

Dr John Sentamu, Archbishop of York

'A prescient and clear book, which will repay careful reading and considered application. The authors are to be congratulated on this excellent, wise and practical guide to ministry.'

The Revd Canon Professor Martyn Percy, Principal,
Ripon College Cuddesdon and The Oxford Ministry Course

'Theologically reflective, sociologically aware and organizationally astute, this eminently practical book is a great companion for all who want to see the importance, value and potential of collaborative ministry realized. Well researched, clearly written, a book by practitioners for practitioners.'

Roy Searle, Leader, Northumbria Community and
former President of the Baptist Union of Great Britain

'This book is well timed, well researched and well expressed. It will give you the tools you need for vision making, team building, understanding group processes, reflective evaluation, facilitation, conflict resolution and effective leadership. Buy it.'

Ray Simpson, Guardian, the International
Community of Aidan and Hilda

'This is a very readable book with helpful practical examples from the authors' own experiences of collaborative working. It is a must for anyone who works with other people – clergy or lay – and particularly those who take a leading role or have the task of managing people. We are all still a work in progress and this book will challenge you to look at yourself and the way you work as you make use of the points for reflection, discussion and action at the end of each chapter. I warmly recommend this book.'

Sonia Barron, National Adviser for the
Committee for Minority Ethnic Anglican Concerns

'Working collaboratively is both theologically sound and pragmatically sensible, yet so many of us struggle with the realities of collaborative ministry. This book is a rich resource to help dispel the myths, shape our understanding, and provide the skills.'

The Revd James Lawrence, Director, CPAS Arrow
Leadership Programme

'One of the great privileges of being the National Director of Youth for Christ is to see the way the Kingdom can be expressed by working collaboratively – through our 67 Centres around the country, and through the partnerships we have seen established through Hope 2008. This confirms to me that we need to find a way to work together to fulfil Jesus' prayer and dream. This book is extremely practical and helpful in achieving that end, and as a partner with the Centre for Youth Ministry this is a demonstration of what can be achieved when groups come together for the Kingdom.'

Roy Crowne, National Director of Youth for Christ

'I overheard a Senior Devil saying to a Junior Devil, "Don't let them collaborate when they can so easily spoil their own ministry with their protective, individualistic, competitive, market-driven, arrogant and stubborn attitudes without our help" – read this book and slough off the plans of hell! It's by people who practise what they preach!'

Dave Wiles, Chief Executive Officer of Frontier Youth Trust

Dr Sally Nash is Director of the Midlands Centre for Youth Ministry, a partnership between St John's, Nottingham, and Youth for Christ. She is a trustee of the Frontier Youth Trust and Sophia, a network for women in youth ministry. She is part of the editorial group for the Grove Booklet Series on leadership and youth, and is currently training for ordination part time. Her publications include *The Faith of Generation Y* and *Tools for Reflective Ministry* (both co-authored), *A Theology for Urban Youth Work* and a range of articles, papers and booklets on spirituality and well-being.

Jo Pimlott, now Jo Whitehead, is Assistant Director of the Midlands Centre for Youth Ministry, where she teaches youth and community work and practical theology and is the community-based pioneer ministry course leader. She has co-authored several books on youth work, including *Inspire, Responding to Challenging Behaviour* and *Youth Work after Christendom*, and is the author of *An Introduction to Managing Yourself*.

The Revd Paul Nash is Senior Chaplain at Birmingham Children's Hospital and a tutor at the Midlands Centre for Youth Ministry. He initiated the Grove Youth Series and has written *What Theology for Youth Work?* He is the author of *Supporting Dying Children and their Families* (2011) and has co-authored *Tools for Reflective Ministry* (2009), both also published by SPCK. He is the cofounder and convener of the Paediatric Chaplaincy Network for Great Britain and Ireland (<http://www.paediatric-chaplaincy-network.org>) and a project leader for Red Balloon Resources (multi-faith paediatric health, palliative and bereavement care, support and training).

SPCK Library of Ministry

BEING A CHAPLAIN
Miranda Threlfall-Holmes and Mark Newitt

COMMUNITY AND MINISTRY: AN INTRODUCTION
TO COMMUNITY DEVELOPMENT IN
A CHRISTIAN CONTEXT
Paul Ballard and Lesley Husselbee

PIONEER MINISTRY AND FRESH EXPRESSIONS
OF CHURCH
Angela Shier-Jones

READER MINISTRY EXPLORED
Cathy Rowling and Paula Gooder

REFLECTIVE CARING: IMAGINATIVE LISTENING
TO PASTORAL EXPERIENCE
Bob Whorton

SKILLS FOR COLLABORATIVE MINISTRY
Sally Nash, Jo Pimlott and Paul Nash

SUPPORTING DYING CHILDREN AND THEIR FAMILIES:
A HANDBOOK FOR CHRISTIAN MINISTRY
Paul Nash

SUPPORTING NEW MINISTERS IN THE LOCAL
CHURCH: A HANDBOOK
Keith Lamdin and David Tilley

TOOLS FOR REFLECTIVE MINISTRY
Sally Nash and Paul Nash

SKILLS FOR COLLABORATIVE MINISTRY

SPCK Library of Ministry

SALLY NASH, JO PIMLOTT
and PAUL NASH

First published in Great Britain in 2008

Society for Promoting Christian Knowledge
36 Causton Street
London SW1P 4ST
www.spck.org.uk

Reissued 2011

British Library Cataloguing-in-Publication Data
A catalogue record for this book is available from the British Library

ISBN 978–0–281–06475–5
eBook ISBN 978–0–281–06608–7

Typeset by Graphicraft Limited, Hong Kong
First printed in Great Britain by Ashford Colour Press
Subsequently digitally printed in Great Britain

eBook by Graphicraft Limited, Hong Kong

Produced on paper from sustainable forests

*This book is dedicated to the students of the
Midlands Centre for Youth Ministry who inspire
and encourage us in our collaborative ministry, and
to all those we have worked with across times and places
from whom we have learnt so much*

Contents

Contents

Contents

Contents

Preface

Collaborative ministry as a term has grown in use and recognition in different parts of the Church over the past 20 or 30 years. This Bible verse offers one of the prime benefits: 'By yourself you're unprotected. With a friend you can face the worst. Can you round up a third? A three-stranded rope isn't easily snapped' (Ecclesiastes 4.12, *The Message*). This is a 'three strand' book, written by people who work together and who represent a range of traditions and perspectives. We were discussing how long we have all been in ministry and scarily we have over 80 years of experience between us although we thought we neither looked nor felt as old as that implies! Between us we have experience in ordained ministry, lay church leadership in both a new church and the Church of England, youth and community work, youth ministry, the voluntary sector, training, adult education, higher education, chaplaincy and denominational structures and all of this in a range of cultural and class settings. We all have a long-term commitment to collaborative ministry and have sought to access and develop skills, knowledge, attitudes and practices that enhance this. We are all practitioners and educators who believe in holistic development and learning. This book reflects who we are and what we believe in and we believe in it passionately enough to want to share something of our journeys and experiences in the hope that it will enhance mission and ministry and enable people to be more effective in their calling.

This is not a book about structures – there is an increasing literature on how to do collaborative ministry (e.g. Christou, 2004; Greenwood, 2000; Robertson, 2007; Whitehead and Whitehead, 1991) – it is a book on the skills that will help you be effective, whatever your structure. The first chapter provides an overview of collaborative ministry drawing on some of the existing literature as well as experience. The second and third chapters on group work processes and facilitation skills are foundational to all the other chapters as they provide underpinning knowledge, understanding and skills for everything that follows. The subsequent chapters look at different skills that help in developing and sustaining collaborative ministry.

Generally we write about experience that is common to all of us; where it specifically draws on one of our contexts we make this clear. Stories in this book are taken from our experiences or experiences shared with us but sometimes details and contexts have been changed to ensure confidentiality. Individuals have taken the lead in different chapters but we have discussed, contributed to and developed each other's thinking; the end product is truly collaborative. As the Japanese proverb says, 'None of us is as smart as all of us.' It is a book you may wish to revisit after you have read it through once and dip in and out of chapters as the issue or need arises.

Sally, Jo and Paul
Holy Island

1

Introduction to collaborative ministry

What is collaborative ministry?

The ancient African proverb, 'It takes a village to raise a child', gives a glimpse of what collaborative ministry can offer – a more holistic, integrated, inclusive way of building the kingdom of God. Another example of collaboration is '*Better Together*', the title of a book written by both the Anglican and Roman Catholic Bishops of Liverpool (Sheppard and Warlock, 1988). Both are great concepts but sometimes delivering true collaboration is hard work. At its best collaborative ministry brings an energy and synergy to what we do and enables us to achieve something we could never have done alone: 'When we collaborate, creativity unfolds across people; the sparks fly faster, and the whole is greater than the sum of its parts' (Sawyer, 2007, p. 7). That's what we hope for! At its worst, collaborative ministry is a nightmare that we wish we had never got into and we fixate on the negative connotations of the word 'collaborator' realizing the mistake we have made.

Books about collaborative ministry reflect some of the ambiguities, ranging from statements such as 'If collaboration means taking others into an open and honest partnership where people and groups co-operate, share strengths and weaknesses, and work towards a common good, then few congregations can say they have approached success' (Nelson, 1996, p. 16). Interestingly, Grundy notes that 'Now this [collaborative ministry] really is a difficult concept for many in the churches' (2007, p. 44) despite saying nine years previously that 'Collaborative ministry is certainly central to the thinking of all who want to see a revitalization of congregational life' (Grundy, 1998, p. 57). One of our observations is that doing collaborative ministry well takes a lot of time and energy in the initial stages before people are able to work together effectively but

1

sometimes people give up prematurely having not persevered through a difficult time and then live with a compromise of a team but not something that is genuinely collaborative.

There are two main types of activity that can be called collaborative. First, a way of working together within an organization or agency and second, working with and alongside other organizations and agencies. Collaborative working has been a trend in both the Church and the caring professions for the last 30 years or so although the concept is being articulated much more clearly now. In our church experience we have heard it called the priesthood of all believers, every-member ministry, team ministry, body ministry, fivefold ministry (based on Ephesians 4.19), shared ministry, local ministry and partnership.

In the caring professions a similar term would be collaborative practice. In this context the terms multiprofessional, multidisciplinary, multiagency are used to describe the way different groups with their specialist knowledge and skills work *alongside* each other to provide services. The terms interprofessional, interdisciplinary and interagency imply that different groups *interact* and learn from each other to improve services (see Payne, 2000). In a church context we do both. Larger churches have a multidisciplinary team where priests or ministers work alongside youth workers, children's workers, evangelists, counsellors, parish nurses and so on. Other churches work in their community and are involved in interagency provision for young people, those who are homeless, people with mental health problems and so on where their professional skills are used alongside those of others who have a responsibility to that community too. Casto gives a rationale for such work:

> Interprofessional practice by those in the helping professions finds its sanction in basic assumptions about the nature of human community and the interdependence of each of us. Whether our responsibilities as pastors and professionals lead us toward the relative isolation of academic work, the passionate response to individuals in crisis in mission work, or the daily routines of the pastorate, we finally discover that our work is dependent on the knowledge, benevolence, and skill of countless others.   (Cited in Lovell, 2000, p. 288)

There is also a wealth of ecumenical work that is genuinely collaborative such as the youth work training undertaken by the

United Reformed Church, Anglicans, Catholics and Methodists in the Northampton area who share resources, finance and leadership at regular training events. Their synergy enabled them to put on wider training events that have equipped over a thousand people involved in youth work.

Business too is realizing that collaborative approaches are vital, for example, 'Collaboration is the premier candidate to replace hierarchy as the organizing principle for leading and managing in the 21st-Century workplace' (Marshall, 1995, p. 4). Here different words are used such as partnership, alliance, network, co-operative, consortium, joint venture, forum, collective as well as collaborative (see Lank, 2006). Collaboration is seen as being about 'more' – being more efficient; getting more sooner; achieving more quality; making more possible; being more committed and unified; gaining more learning (Perkins, 2003, p. 157). Elements of many of these may be why in our context we want to explore and develop collaborative ministry.

Although we are focusing on collaborative ministry we hope that the material will also be of use to people in other sectors who are involved in collaborative practice of one form or another. Our definition of collaborative ministry is an approach that:

- recognizes and acknowledges that there are a diversity of gifts and vocations within the body of Christ which need to be identified and nurtured so that all can play their part;
- believes that reflecting the nature of God and Christ's example requires interdependence and a willingness to work together over-coming barriers and conflict;
- shares a commitment to a common purpose, vision and mission;
- takes seriously shared decision-making and a devolution of power and authority.

As with most of what we hear, we filter the term 'collaborative ministry' through our own ears. Sally is very committed to collaborative ministry but often interprets it as working on her own doing her part towards the whole. Paul's preference is often the opposite and he sees collaborative ministry as doing the work together and often wants to discuss everything with everyone. The way we edited this book was probably Jo's preferred way. We discussed all the chapters and got an overview of what was needed to be done, we then worked individually on laptops in the same room with the capacity to ask each other

3

for help and ideas. One of the first things we needed to do was to make sure there was a shared perspective on the team or at least an understanding of how each other will work best.

Theological perspectives

A fundamental argument for collaborative ministry is that God collaborates with us and that this is the pattern we are offered in the New Testament. This is Robertson's (2007) starting point but he also explores a range of predominantly ecclesiological perspectives and demonstrates how they relate to collaborative ministry. Another perspective is based around unity, the first quotation in *The Sign We Give* (1995), a Roman Catholic report on collaborative ministry, is:

> I have given them the glory you gave to me, that they may be one as we are one. With me in them and you in me, may they be so perfected in unity that the world will recognise that it was you who sent me and that you have loved them as you loved me.   (John 17.22–23)

The Church of England suggests that 'Collaboration in ministry is, in the first instance, collaboration with God in the *missio dei* [mission of God]' (Church of England, 2003, p. 3). Carter uses 'body theology' and argues that 'the church is the sum of its members' gifts' and that gifts should not be distinguished in value as all are both necessary and important regardless of whether the community or individual sees them as such. He concludes that 'Ministry is the function of the whole body in which each member has an irreplaceable role' (1997, pp. 17–18).

Trinitarian perspectives are also common and have been used in ecumenical, denominational and diocesan discussions on ministry (Greenwood, 2002, pp. 82–3), and it is this perspective that we will explore further. Collaboration is at the heart of the nature of our Trinitarian God. *The Message* version of Isaiah 2.3 encapsulates what this means: 'He'll show us the way he works so we can live the way we're made', which we take to mean that we're made to work in community, collaboratively. In collaborative ministry we work together, bringing our different gifts and attributes, our complementary callings and vocations. The Trinity gives us an example of synergy, the whole is greater than the sum of the parts. However, each part has a distinct role and is committed to working together both within and outside of themselves. There is an equality at the heart of the Trinity that we would do well to imitate, treating each other with respect, seeing the good in each other, valuing the diversity. There are no power plays in the Trinity, there are interactions between persons of equal worth. If collaboration is going to work then this is the attitude we need to adopt. The differences in the roles and functions of the Trinity should inspire us to see tension as a creative force but to strive for a harmony. An excellent summary of a Trinitarian understanding of partnership and collaboration is that used by the group Christians in Public Life:

- We are called to be partners with God in his continuing work of creating with the personal, corporate and global spheres of life.
- We are called to be partners with Christ as he frees and empowers individuals, institutions and nations to fulfil their God-given possibilities.
- We are called to be partners with the Spirit as she works for justice, peace and the unity of mankind.
- We are called to be partners with all those who work to further human dignity within the bounds of our common humanity (Cited in Clark, 1996, p. 69).

Some denominational perspectives on collaborative ministry

Greenwood, writing from an Anglican perspective, describes how ministry moves from predominantly one person to something more collaborative:

Model One – the collusion that the clergy (plus licensed others) are to provide professional services for people, such as leading worship, visiting, preaching, and so on

Model Two – because the vicar is ill or has too much to do, others – by delegation – are sometimes 'allowed to help' him/her in carefully supervised ways

Model Three – all Christians by baptism share Christ's ministry for the world. This is a church of, not just for, people. The priest is actually

called to be a minister of unity, allowing for the mutuality of difference in relation. The priest 'holds the ring' (presides/oversees) in that
(s)he invokes in all ministries that which gives the church its specific
missionary character – holiness, catholicity and apostolicity.

(2000, pp. 34–5)

To engage in genuinely collaborative ministry, rather than just have
more people doing the jobs that one person used to do, requires
an underpinning theology of ministry and perhaps a willingness to
listen to the perspectives of people from other disciplines who may
be more familiar with this approach. For example, one of the first
things that we teach our youth workers are the four principles of
(secular) good youth work practice: being educative, empowering,
participative and committed to equal opportunities (see Brierley,
2003, for an explanation and critique of them). In this understanding,
participative means sharing in the decision-making and power structures of the work rather than just taking part. Such principles lend
themselves well to collaborative ministry. Community work, similarly,
would have an underlying philosophy that complements the idea of
shared working: 'Community work is about the active involvement
of people in the issues which affect their lives and focuses on the
relationship between individuals and groups and the institutions
which shape their everyday experience' (Harris, 2001, p. 1). In writing
about ministry, Lovell suggests that 'An inescapable conclusion of any
examination of church work is that collaboration is written deep into
its nature' (2000, p. 287). He notes, however, that actual practice does
not necessarily reflect this, and that:

> Not only have large sections of it [the Church] neglected collabora-
> tion, some have argued against it, tried to undermine theologically those
> practising it and strenuously promoted non-participatory and hier-
> archical approaches and structures. Yet others have been calculatedly
> manipulative. Some clergy resist it on theological grounds, arguing that
> leaders called by God and ordained by the Church must lead and
> followers must follow. Others resist it on practical and psychological
> grounds, e.g. it takes too much time, the fear of loss of control.
>
> (Lovell, 2000, p. 287)

Different parts of the Church are exploring collaborative ministry.
In 1995 a significant Roman Catholic report was published which
offered a definition of collaborative ministry framed in terms of

principles and convictions; below are those which seem more widely applicable:

- Collaborative ministry is a way of relating and working together in the life of the Church which expresses the communion which the Church is given and to which it is called. It is a way of working in which the quality of relationships developed is as important as the task in which we are engaged.
- Involvement in collaborative ministry demands conscious commitment to certain values and convictions. These include a recognition that Christian initiation gives us a shared but differentiated responsibility for the life and mission of the Church, and calls us to work together on equal terms; the conviction that our different vocations and gifts are complementary and mutually enriching; an agreement that we are accountable to each other for how we work and what we do.
- Collaborative ministry begins from a fundamental desire to work together because we are called by the Lord to be a company of disciples, not isolated individuals. It grows through a mutual process of conversion and formation. It also requires a willingness to face and work through conflict because of the attraction and value of a common good, supported by an awareness of participating in the work of the Spirit in the Church.
- Collaborative ministry is ministry committed to mission. It is not simply concerned with the internal life of the Church. Rather, it shows to the world the possibility of transformation, of community and of unity within diversity (Bishop's Conference of England and Wales, 1995).

The final paragraph of an Anglican document on collaborative ministry in mission provides a helpful insight that would ensure that collaborative ministry began in the right way:

> If the quality of collaboration is to reflect the relationships we perceive within the Trinity and if it is to be true to the model that Paul offers us in 1 Corinthians, then it must be collaborative in its conception as well as in its life. 'Let us pray' followed by 'let us . . . together' is the way forward, rather than 'I have decided . . . will you . . . ?'
> (Board of Mission, 1995, p. 53)

Anglican Franciscans have explored the relevance of collaborative ministry and Burrows concludes that 'There is a genuine Franciscan tradition that sees ministry as an activity to which all brothers and sisters are called, though the pattern of that ministry will vary between individuals because of vocation, context and opportunity' (2005, p. 3).

From a caring professions perspective, collaborative teams are seen as a way of delivering more holistic care. Such teams are built around:

> shared vision, based on beliefs and values about responding to people's needs. Work is managed primarily on the basis of shared vision whereby contribution to realising the vision is understood, valued and based on mutual role responsibility and genuine collaboration.
>
> (Johns, 2004, p. 171)

What's in a name?

What we call our collaborative ministry will often say something about our values and structure. Whitehead and Whitehead differentiate between the terms staff, team and community while acknowledging that sometimes they are used interchangeably (1991, pp. 52–9). Staff means a work group with differing levels of responsibility; its strengths are order and efficiency but the challenges are to keep the structure flexible and to encourage connections between staff members as well as the staff member and leader. Team is an interdependent, mutually accountable group which has complementary strengths and can be flexible and spontaneous; challenges are establishing effective working patterns and structures. Community is a group which shares values, nurtures a common vision, has a mutual concern and undertakes common action; they are mutually supportive but a challenge is to move values into action and balance belonging with effectiveness. We need to think carefully about what we call our collaborative ministry as terms come with meanings, sometimes with baggage, and can influence how we operate and how we are perceived. We recommend spending time together reflecting on what the ministry is called and how this may impact the functioning of the team and whether this facilitates or hinders a collaborative approach to ministry. If we don't do this we may fall into a way of working anyway by default or influenced by the leader or strongest personalities on the team.

What are the qualities of a collaborative worker?

The answer to this question partly depends on who we are trying to collaborate with and our own personality. Qualities we value are being self-aware, having a servant heart, knowing our limitations, expecting the best of others, giving of our best, being facilitative in approach, keeping our word, listening, being willing to take risks, commitment to the process and building a shared vision. In working with others in collaborative ministry what we find helpful is being listened to, our expertise being respected, a willingness to take the time to gain a shared perspective and make a genuinely collaborative decision, giving time and attention to developing process as well as wanting to achieve outcomes.

Frontier Youth Trust is an organization whose main approach to work is collaborative. They have a significant number of partnerships with different agencies delivering training, youth work and support (see <www.fyt.org.uk>). Dave Wiles, the Chief Executive, identifies some of the key qualities that in his experience are needed; such qualities may be spread around the team:

- ability to inspire and enthuse disparate world views, values and beliefs – good communication skills help with this;
- conciliation and reconciliation skills – to ensure that the past receives enough attention without blocking the future;
- groupwork skills – an ability to give balanced attention to the task–process balance in groups;
- enabling people to celebrate what they have achieved, to learn from it and to build a group consciousness that ensures ongoing collaboration;
- enabling reviews which ensure the perpetual scope for reformation that adapts what gets done in the future and who can be involved;
- non-defensive perspective on theology and beliefs – be clear about what is important and forget the rest – it only leads to fights.

Sometimes we can define what we are looking for by identifying the opposite. Lank (2006, p. 129) identifies the nightmare partner as one who is status-conscious, arrogant, has a strong need for structure, is uncomfortable with change, focuses on their personal agenda, is not curious about different ways of approaching things, takes a win–lose rather than a win–win approach and is a poor listener.

There are attitudes and approaches which are supportive of collaborative ministry and are likely to make it more effective. A foundational one is an understanding of roles and expertise, particularly in interprofessional work, along with a respect for those roles. This is not always the case; for instance, Crystal, a youth worker, describes how, when she said she was going to get ordained as a Baptist youth specialist, two of the local Anglican clergy seemed to view her more positively as if they suddenly knew what sort of a 'minister' she was. They understood the language of ordination but were less familiar with the idea of a secularly qualified professional youth worker based in the church who expected to be treated as an equal. Even when we are attempting to be non-hierarchical there can often be an informal or perceived hierarchy where some roles or tasks are deemed to be more important than others. This is when confidence can be important, if we are confident in our own role then we are more likely to serve in that role in a way that is helpful and non-threatening. A basic commitment to this way of working is vital, otherwise there will be a series of road blocks which prevent effective working. Honest communication is needed for collaboration to be effective and that means being open to listen, to give and receive feedback, to be willing to contribute positively to the process. Time for both social activities and reflection aids relationships and understanding. Praying together (where this is appropriate and being sensitive to tradition) as well as working together helps maintain the ultimate focus of the collaboration.

Barriers to collaborative ministry

One of the barriers to effective collaborative ministry is that we may not have the skills needed to work in this way. Hierarchical models of church leadership and what seems to be an inbuilt deference to those who are ordained also make it difficult for genuine collaborative ministry to take place. It needs a degree of security and confidence to change traditional ways of working and help us to understand ideas of shared responsibility as something positive rather than something that feels like another burden to bear (because of time, low self-esteem, consumerist views of Church, for example). A lack of willingness to deal with conflict also means that attempts at collaborative ministry may come to a premature end (see Chapter 8 on conflict for help with this). True collaborative ministry needs to move beyond super-ficial relationships and it would be unusual for this to take place with-out going through at least some conflict. Bad experiences from the past often stop us initiating or participating in collaborative min-istry as does arrogance or an unwillingness to engage with people who are different (see Chapter 9 on diversity). Issues around power can be a barrier too; unless we are willing to share power and be accountable it can be difficult to achieve genuine collaborative min-istry. An issue related to this is when we have our own agenda which we pursue outside the stated purpose of the collaboration. Barriers can come both from a leader unwilling to give up their power or team members who are unwilling to take the power that a leader is trying to share. Mutual accountability is a quality to pursue.

In an interprofessional context, Freeth (2001, p. 44) identifies some of the challenges to sustaining the work:

> structural differences between organizations, conflicting organiza-tional and professional agendas, resource requirements, more complex communication demands, replacing former team members, induct-ing and forming strong links with new team members, regular evalu-ation and shared planning of the team's shared goals and progress.

With collaboration outside of the Church or agency these are some of the potential barriers that will need to be explored and addressed. Putting sufficient time into establishing the working relationship early on may help this approach be accepted more readily with people willing to make enough effort to ensure that it succeeds. How-ever, collaborative working between churches and other agencies is still problematic in some areas with the Church regarded with some suspicion, and certainly in the youth work field, seen as not neces-sarily doing 'proper' youth work. Leona tells her story:

> When I started at the council youth club I was regarded with some suspicion for quite some time and only by staying and working well did I earn some respect. I think the fact that I was doing a JNC (secular professional youth work qualification) course helped as well – I'm now better qualified than the senior youth worker! I think they still tend to disregard my separate activities as youth work in the sense they understand it – they make no effort to collaborate, and don't visit our projects. When I went out round the village with the team on a detached session looking to make contact with young people on

the streets the leader in charge ignored my comments about where the young people usually hang out, despite knowing that I have lived in the village for 13 years. They seem to assume that they are the ones doing the serious stuff and us church folk are just messing about on the edges.

Leadership in collaborative ministry

In collaborative ministry there will usually need to be a leader. Often attempts to work in a more egalitarian way mean that a 'shadow' leader emerges who adopts the role (or is forced into the role) without this being properly acknowledged, which can create tensions and dissatisfaction for those in the team as well as confusion for those on the outside. One of the key questions to ask about leadership in collaborative ministry is whether we lead in our natural style or lead in the way that is most appropriate for the situation or team. Leadership can make or break teams and Sally's experience and research suggests that youth workers most often leave a job prematurely because they don't get on with the leader of the church or project. Whether a volunteer joins a collaborative ministry team or not may well depend on the quality of leadership. For collaborative ministry to be at its most effective careful attention needs to be given to leadership. Leadership is a complex and often contested concept. If we search Amazon for books on leadership we will find enough to read a book a day for the rest of our lives! Leadership is about who we are, what we are trying to achieve, and how we are going to get it done. In collaborative ministry what we are trying to achieve and how we are going to get it done may be best worked out with others in the team. But openness to this idea may depend on who we are and our natural style. Broadly there is a spectrum of leadership between laissez-faire and autocratic which is explored in Table 1.1.

Whatever leadership style we adopt there are three main needs, identified by Adair (1997, p. 16), that the leader needs to ensure are met:

- task need – getting the job done;
- team maintenance need – creating and developing a cohesive group;
- individual need – paying attention to physical, psychological, social, emotional and spiritual needs.

Table 1.1 Leadership style and implications for collaborative ministry

Leadership style	Implications for collaborative ministry
Laissez-faire	In laissez-faire leadership the leader functions more as a peer and has little authority. This style can work with a highly motivated team who like to be quite autonomous. However, it can lead to confusion on the part of team members as they are offered little support and there is little structure. They may feel there is a lack of identity or purpose and feel a little insecure or frustrated.
Democratic	Democratic leadership is exercised by people who seek to be inclusive and to develop a team which feels empowered. They share decision-making and encourage a degree of independence in their team. For many people this will result in commitment, motivation and a sense of purpose. A possible danger is that too much participation encourages power plays or a tendency to make popular decisions that may not be right.
Charismatic	Charismatic leaders often rely on their personality to make things happen. There may be little structure and some team members may feel insecure, not knowing what is expected of them, or unclear about a vision which can keep changing. A danger of this style is subgroups and feelings of inclusion and exclusion depending on a team member's relationship with the leader.
Benevolent	Benevolent leaders tend to provide a clear structure and operate with clear lines of accountability. It can feel paternalistic to more independent team members and encourage dependence on the leader in others. It is an approach that can feel comfortable in a church setting because it has a family feel; however, it may not function as efficiently as it could do because of the desire to keep everyone happy.
Autocratic	Autocratic leaders control the group, tend to issue orders and believe that any questioning of them is not appropriate behaviour. The leader resists participation and is often unaccountable. It is a way of leading that is an antithesis of collaborative ministry as it discourages people from taking responsibility for themselves and suppresses creativity and initiative-taking.

For effective collaborative ministry all three of these need to be held in tension and worked on. Figure 1.1 identifies Adair's functions of a leader.

Figure 1.1 Functions of a leader according to Adair (1997)

It is helpful for us to reflect on how we would draw these circles in relation to each other in our experience of collaborative ministry. In our experience, difficulties and issues can be dealt with more effectively and honestly if there is a more even balance. It can be hard with the busyness of people's lives to argue that we need to spend time getting to know each other but beginning to know and trust each other may help us function more effectively more quickly. We have sometimes found a reluctance to offer one-to-one meetings within collaborative ministry teams but these can be vital for individual development and for people to feel affirmed.

In reflecting on the approach to leadership in collaborative ministry Warren has identified five key movements away from traditional practice:

- being a conductor rather than a director – building on the gifts within the church rather than on those of the minister;
- becoming a facilitator rather than a provider – enabling people to do for themselves rather than adopting a client mode;
- permission-giver rather than permission-withholder – allowing laity to shape and initiate;
- steering rather than rowing – causing everything to be done as opposed to doing everything;

- being a person rather than a parson – being human is a reflection of the incarnate Christ and being open and vulnerable contributes to this (Board of Mission, 1995, pp. 25–6).

The values are perhaps more widely accepted than when first written but there may also need to be a paradigm shift in the views of laity who may approach church with a consumer mentality or, as we have heard said, 'We pay them, why should we do it?' Building shared understandings of leadership is an essential early step in developing more collaborative styles of ministry. Perhaps the first step as a leader is to help people develop a sense of belonging and ownership of the concept and team. To belong means to feel included and participate actively, which enhances a sense of self and brings out the best which in turn engenders a willingness to give to the group (Whitehead and Whitehead, 1991, p. 105).

Conclusion

This chapter has given an introduction to the concept of collaborative ministry and identified some of the issues that need to be thought through when introducing the approach. Subsequent chapters explore the key skills needed to be effective in collaborative ministry and offer ideas and tools for different facets of what we do.

Points for reflection, discussion and action

- What is your instinctive reaction to the idea of collaborative ministry? What are the roots of this reaction?
- Why do you want to explore and develop collaborative ministry in your setting?
- What are the key principles for collaborative ministry that resonate with you in your context?
- If you are already involved in collaborative ministry, what barriers have you faced and how have you sought to overcome them?
- How do the structures of your church or agency facilitate or mitigate against collaborative ministry?
- Which of the models of leadership are most prevalent in your context? Are there any changes that would make collaborative ministry more effective?

- Which theological underpinning for collaborative ministry attracts you most?
- Have any new insights struck you as you have been reading this chapter?
- Who do you want to meet with to discuss introducing or developing collaborative ministry in your context?

2

Groupwork processes for collaborative ministry

> The need to stand alone. The need to belong. How do you hold them together? (Riddell, 1997, p. 62)

An understanding of group process is essential to anyone involved in collaborative ministry, not least because the moment we begin to work with others in any structured way we create a group of some kind. Additionally, much collaborative ministry will take place in group contexts. These groups may be diverse in terms of focus (like Bible study, prayer, support, pastoral care, friendship, discussion, evangelism) or a specific function or ministry (like youth work, worship, administration, leadership, catering). Some speak of groups and teams interchangeably. We approach them separately, although much of the material in this chapter and Chapter 6 on Teamwork skills is relevant and can be applied to the other. (For more on the differences between a group and a team see pp. 77–8.) A working understanding of group processes provides an important foundation, underpinning many of the subsequent skills required for collaborative ministry.

What is a group?

Much has been written on the subject of groups and a plethora of definitions exist, which address the subject on different levels. At its simplest a group is a collection or gathering of people who interact, have certain characteristics in common or share a common identity. In Christian contexts we will find ourselves working in various sized groups. Congregations are examples of larger groups and many churches will have meetings of smaller gatherings for various purposes. Indeed, the small group has been described as 'the basic building block of the life of the local congregation and is fundamental to the development of individual and corporate Christian lifestyle' (Mallison, 1996, p. 1).

Groups will be structured in different ways depending on their purpose and context. They may be formal or informal, gathered or networked, flat or hierarchical. We see groups as dynamic, organic and multifaceted. They are complex and constantly changing, as the people within them bring who they are, who they are becoming, their opinions, interests, skills, values, experiences, responses and learning. We also believe that a group is more than the sum of the individuals that comprise it and that dynamics within some groups create what might be described as a 'group-as-a-whole' entity (Ringer, 2002, p. 146). This basically means that the group can take on a life of its own and create its own patterns of behaviour, thinking and responding. This is slightly different from the way in which individuals might change their behaviour in different groups they belong to, and will be explored more fully later in this chapter.

It is important to recognize external factors that might influence or affect groups – groups do not exist in a vacuum and they can be affected by an array of contextual factors.

> I think of groups as small social units that develop their own ways of communicating, creating meaning and taking action. Furthermore, each group is situated in the context of complex organizational, cultural and social milieux. So the study of groups becomes the study of small complex dynamic social systems where the leader is an integral part of that system and factors outside the immediate group are considered to be relevant. (Ringer, 2002, pp. 17–18)

Stages of group development

Those working with groups need to be aware that groups go through life cycles or stages of development. Tuckman's work on this in the 1960s has provided the foundation for much of the current thinking around this issue. His research originally identified four stages: forming, storming, norming and performing, although others have added a fifth stage to do with ending groups – often referred to as mourning or adjourning.

Forming

The forming stage involves the group coming together and becoming a cohesive whole. Members of the new group may be tentative and their own individual needs tend to be in the forefront of people's minds as they are often preoccupied with questions of how they will fit, what others might think of them, whether they really want to be there and how the group is going to feel for them. They may be uncertain about the group's purpose or about other group members and there is often a strong sense of dependence on any authority figure within the group – whether they are the 'official' group leader or not.

Those leading or facilitating groups in this stage should allow people opportunity to interact socially. Light refreshments can help, as can space for informal chat, although informal icebreakers may also be appropriate in some contexts. When using icebreakers it is important to choose activities which won't embarrass group members, such as over-silly games, difficult-to-answer puzzles or extremely personal questions. An ideal icebreaker will be fun but will not over-expose participants, finding ways of encouraging everyone to have a voice, without pressuring people to say or reveal more than they want to.

It is important at the outset to also agree boundaries and expectations, ideally through discussion and negotiation with the whole group. This process is commonly referred to as contracting and might cover issues like attendance, punctuality, confidentiality and boundaries around listening to one another or respecting different viewpoints. It is also vital to clarify the reasons for and purpose of the group, exploring what will happen and the intention of any task involved.

This will normally be done informally through conversation and discussion with the group. We would not usually use formal language for this – words like 'contracting' or 'ground rules' – but would generally open the conversation by asking questions such as 'How do we want to work as a group together today?' or 'What things are important to each of us in terms of how we respond to one another?' Sometimes it is helpful to write responses up on a flip chart. At other times it is enough simply to give space to highlighting and exploring them.

At the forming stage, group culture and norms begin to be established, so those with responsibility should be aware of what they are looking to see develop. For example, if we want people to be involved in taking responsibility and making decisions we need to implement this straight away to set a precedent for the future.

Group leaders should recognize that people may bring baggage from previous groups or experiences with them into the new group. For example, in learning groups participants often bring both positive and negative earlier experiences of education. For some this will mean that they come expecting to sit and listen or to feel embarrassed and stupid. If members of the group already know each other, which is common in church-based groups, it is important to recognize that 'past history' can affect this stage of the group quite significantly (Brown, 1994, p. 102).

Although this stage occurs at the beginning of the group's life cycle, to a certain extent forming will take place every time the group gets together and will certainly happen if someone new joins. Even a latecomer can 'send' a group back into the forming stage and we need to be aware of this.

Storming

At this stage group members begin to feel less wary and let their guard down a little. This is a time of checking people out and testing to see where the boundaries are – whether it is a safe place to be. Some people might try and dominate during this phase, others will assert their individuality more, clarifying where they differ from others. These differences can sometimes be seen as 'all or nothing, for or against' (Jaques, 1992, p. 34) and can create tension and friction. This can feel uncomfortable but it is an important part of group development.

Often those responsible for groups struggle to allow and give space for storming, perhaps because they themselves feel anxious or because they sense and are concerned about the anxiety in the group. This can be an issue in Christian groups in particular, where conflict is often seen as purely negative and facilitators placate and intervene, rather than allowing storming to take place. Getting the balance right is important. If leadership is too directive in this phase it can encourage passivity and dependence, but if the storming phase continues too long it can prevent the group achieving anything at all and can be emotionally draining. Facilitators need to lead strongly enough to create clear boundaries and build security, but should not be over-directive. Creating safe spaces is really important, as is encouraging group members to listen to each other and seeking to handle feedback, discussion and negotiation effectively. The skills outlined in Chapters 3 and 8 on facilitation and conflict respectively should be particularly useful here.

Sometimes storming can become self-directed and may manifest in individual group members as depression if, for example, individuals' (perhaps unrealistic) hopes and expectations of the group fail to be met (Brown, 1994, p. 105).

Most groups will storm naturally, even if it is rather tentatively and politely. When a group does not storm or appears to be deliberately avoiding disagreement, we can provide structured opportunities for this to happen. This can help the group feel 'safer' about storming. Jo has sometimes staged a debate on an issue, allocating views and perspectives which individuals research and then 'argue'. In this way, people can argue with the focus firmly on the issue rather than the person – having no emotional investment in their argument means they can 'practise' storming without fearing personal criticism or rejection. Such approaches can get people out of passivity, clear the air and give opportunities for individuals to practise skills in terms of framing and articulating their opinions within the group.

Norming

During the norming stage, the emphasis moves away from the pre-occupations with individual concerns of group members to mutual concerns and a sense of interrelating. Group norms (accepted ways of behaving and relating) really begin to emerge at this stage with a growing sense of collaboration, listening and enquiry. Co-operation and negotiation continue to be important and facilitators need to be aware of the group norms which are emerging – as some may not be positive and may need to be addressed.

Normally during this stage the group should begin to move towards the task focus. This can be challenging as members are often developing a strong emotional investment into the group, and there is a danger of it becoming quite self-absorbed. There is also a risk of established 'norms' stifling or limiting the group's creativity. Where discussion is flowing well a group leader may choose to take a back seat in this stage, allowing the group to function and intervening only occasionally to give suggestions and provide support.

Performing

Although performing usually begins during the norming stage, the group should gradually move into a place where this is the usual way the group works (Brown, 1994, p. 108). Here the group moves into more task-oriented functioning, with people settled into established roles and feeling they know where they fit. At this stage the group acquires a real sense of its own culture (Jaques, 1992, p. 34). Normally group leaders can adopt more of a facilitative role, functioning increasingly as group members and gradually allowing the group to 'manage' itself as people take responsibility for their roles and tasks. Facilitators may need to support or intervene if the group falls back into one of the other stages.

Because of the sense of cohesion and effective functioning that marks the group at this stage, this is often a difficult time for new people to join and care needs to be taken to effectively integrate new or potential members.

Mourning (or adjourning)

Some groups will be open-ended. Others will agree to meet for a defined period and then close. It has been argued that time-limited groups often have a clearer sense of direction and achieve their goals more effectively than open-ended ones (Manor, 2000, p. 36). Whatever the structure of the group in this sense, at some point, the group is likely to end.

This fifth stage is an important one, which is often neglected. We have been in many contexts where groups have ended, died or been 'killed off' with no acknowledgement or marking of this. We need to recognize that people may feel very differently about the group ending, depending on their personal investment in it, the reasons for the ending, any achievements or disappointments and the relational closeness that exists. Facilitators have a significant role here in managing the process of closing the group.

Finding appropriate methods or tools to effectively do this is crucial. These will vary depending on the circumstances, but Mallinson (1996, p. 157) helpfully suggests five important aspects of closure, which inform our approach. These are recalling (high points, helpful things, encouragements), confession (brief acknowledgement of areas where hurt might have occurred), thanksgiving (can be done creatively), expressions of hope (for future personally, for the work, ministry, etc.) and farewell. Allowing space for these things should ensure people are able to move on as healthily as possible.

Joining groups

At this point it is worth mentioning the dynamics that occur when newcomers join an existing group. The group's initial response will depend on numerous factors, including the newcomer's personality – shy, outgoing or aggressive – the stage of the group's development and whether the people who make up the existing group are welcoming or not. The group's history and any preconceived ideas or experience of the newcomer may also be significant.

Normally the group will return to a forming stage, which may last a longer or shorter time, depending on how the new person fits, allowing existing group members another chance to rehearse some of the forming issues, while discovering whether the newcomer can be trusted. The group may create an informal 'probation' period for the newcomer. If the group is in a vulnerable place and the newcomer appears dominant or aggressive, they may be met with suspicion and hostility. Conversely, if the group is already well integrated, a newcomer may be welcomed warmly. The group will feel 'strange' until the newcomer is integrated and this sense of strangeness will encourage the newcomer to understand the group's norms and culture and to fit in.

Group norms and culture

Whenever anyone joins a group, a form of socialization takes place. Socialization has been described as 'the process through which an individual learns to be a member of society' (Berger, 1972, p. 62). This occurs first in childhood – through 'primary socialization' – and then subsequently, though less intensely, throughout life as the individual joins new social groups – 'secondary socialization' (Berger and Luckmann, 1966). Theorists suggest the willingness to adapt our identity to 'fit' the social groups of which we are a part reflects an innate desire to belong and to be able to self-define in a way that makes sense to us. To a certain extent, throughout life, we are constantly adapting and changing our identities to conform to the changing social groups in which we find ourselves. Much of the time this is done unconsciously or, at best, half-consciously.

Socialization in groups manifests itself through the development of group norms. Group norms 'specify, more or less precisely, certain rules for how group members should behave and thus are the basis for mutual expectations amongst the group members' (Brown, 1988, p. 42). Group norms are important for individuals within the group in helping them have a sense of security and knowing what is expected. They also serve to give identity and cohesion to the group and often enable it to function effectively as a social unit from a task perspective. Those joining groups will often quickly learn what is expected by observing behaviour and listening to interactions. In many churches, for example, there are numerous unwritten 'rules', which people learn through their belonging but which might not be articulated or spelt out. At our workplace, for example, we stand to say Grace before lunch, but we sometimes forget to brief visitors about this and they automatically come in and sit down, which often makes them feel awkward because they are not fitting in with group norms.

Organizational culture

Thus, groups and organizations we belong to exercise a strong influence over our behaviour and even our values. This works very powerfully in organizations, where organizational (or even denominational) norms can be very strongly in place and difficult to shift and move.

On one occasion Jo and her husband Nigel were invited to lead a service in a Pentecostal church, in which they had often led meetings and preached. On this occasion the service included Communion. Both were experienced in leading such services, and this time Jo led that part of the morning. After the service they discovered that it was the first time a woman had ever led Communion in the church. Because the church generally had a positive view of women in ministry, Jo and Nigel had not even considered asking the question. In subsequent conversations it emerged that no one had a particular issue with it theologically, no one even strongly objected to Jo doing it, but there was a lot of surprise that it had happened. It had simply become ingrained in the culture of the church that a man always led that part of the service.

Whatever agency – church, project, charity, business, school – we might be involved in at any point in time, it will have its own unique identity and culture. Charles Handy, who has written extensively on organizational culture, highlights the importance of recognizing this diversity: 'For organizations are as different and varied as the nations and societies of the world. They have differing cultures and sets of values and norms and beliefs – reflected in different structures and systems' (Handy, 1993, p. 180).

An organization's culture will often not be acknowledged or recognized, but is likely to influence all areas of its thinking and working, so it is imperative that we are aware of these issues when looking at group processes and at broader issues around collaborative ministry. Handy (1993, p. 180) highlights four different types of cultures which exist in organizations.

Power culture

Organizations with this culture tend to be relatively small and entrepreneurial. Handy's image for this type of culture is the spider's web with a key figure sitting at the centre – usually a leader. The organization is based on relationship, communication is oral rather than written and emphasis is on leadership rather than management. Organizations with a power culture can feel quite personal and tend to have a strong sense of identity. However, it can be frustrating for those who are not 'in' with the central figure and can struggle communication-wise as the organization grows. Many churches which have one key leader are power cultures.

Role culture

This type of culture is more functional and places emphasis on management rather than leadership. It tends to encourage strategy and process and creates systems for ensuring that work is completed efficiently and effectively. Individuals within the organization occupy roles, which may change as the priorities of the organization change.

Organizations with a role culture thrive when doing routine and ongoing work, have an emphasis on training and are efficient. At times though they can feel impersonal, they may struggle with change and they do not encourage individuality or entrepreneurial approaches.

Task culture

Organizations with a task culture tend to be dynamic, creative and forward-thinking. They are often structured around people working in groups to achieve specific tasks and emphasize the importance of sharing skills and responsibilities. They will tend to be non-hierarchical, using facilitative approaches and are co-operative and relational. They encourage personal development but don't cope well with routine or repetition. They can also waste time on discussing, envisioning, exploring and reinventing and can feel quite threatening to people who are less confident and prefer more security.

Person culture

Organizations with a person culture are not as common as the other three and tend to see administration and management as less important and those functions often having lower status. Examples of person cultures can be found in law firms, doctors' surgeries and universities. The organization is seen as a resource for the talents of the key individuals and for these people this culture works well. Administratively this culture is more challenging as it is run more through persuasion rather than authority.

This way of seeing organizational culture is helpful within collaborative ministry settings as it may give us insight into the way our church or organization operates. There may be conflict between preferred approaches and there are obvious implications for working across organizational boundaries. Collaborative work involving people from different agencies will often mean that several contrasting cultures come into play. This may result in clashes of style and approach. Being explicit about identifying and engaging with organizational and group culture will assist in working through such challenges.

Group roles and behaviour

Roles can be ascribed formally within groups, relating to particular jobs or tasks, or may be adopted intentionally or unconsciously by group members. These roles then determine how individuals might behave or act within the group. Whether prescribed or not, roles give individuals a sense of security and identity as, like group norms, they 'imply expectations about one's own and others' behaviour and this means that group life becomes more predictable and hence more orderly' (Brown, 1988, p. 55).

The different ways in which groups and members of groups function can be classified as either group maintenance or task-oriented roles (Jaques, 1984, p. 28). Those who adopt group mainten-ance roles might encourage other group members, mediate in disputes, contribute to discussion, welcome or care for others and relieve tension through humour. Task functions include initiating discussion, giving information or opinions, making suggestions, clarifying points, co-ordinating, leading, keeping the group focused on the task or summarizing and drawing things together.

Some people might commonly adopt a particular role regularly within a group, others may change roles within relatively short periods. People can also adopt different types of role in different groups they belong to. Some adopted roles or behaviours can chal-lenge group facilitators, although most roles are neither inherently positive nor negative but depend on the context. Some people end up getting 'stuck' in a particular role. Gary, a member of a team Jo used to lead a number of years ago, one day shared his frustration that no one ever asked him to pray or sought his input or advice. He had a lot of wisdom and experience, cared for others and was a mature Christian. However, because he had become 'stuck' in the role of clown others simply did not expect him to input in other ways. It was only when Gary shared his feelings with the group that things began to change.

Group dynamics

Issues of group dynamics are complex and multifaceted. Although some aspects of group dynamics will be self-evident, others will re-quire a high degree of experience and understanding to identify and address.

Subgrouping

Every group has actual or potential subgroups. Subgrouping happens when groups split into smaller units in response to something that happens. Subgroups are usually based on a sense of similarity – either real or perceived, or on shared interests or opinions. Some unhealthy group dynamics can result as it can lead to competitiveness between subgroups undermining the effectiveness of a group or to labelling or scapegoating. For example, in one youth group some members of the group became labelled as the 'swots'. Anyone who sat with them or spent time with them was perceived in this way.

Scapegoating

In Leviticus the scapegoat was used by the people of Israel as a recipient for all their sins (Leviticus 16.8–10). In groups, the scapegoat becomes the focus of the group's stresses or anxieties, often being blamed for things or receiving significant negative attention and thus enabling the group to avoid real issues. Interestingly, scapegoats often accept their role without defending themselves, suggesting that this role satisfies them in some way (Brown, 1994, p. 126). Scapegoating can be addressed directly through intervening to challenge it, for example, drawing attention to the fact that 'Chris seems to be getting a lot of stick today' or indirectly by using processes which break down the group into smaller units and change the processes of interaction.

Rescuing

Rescuing describes behaviour where someone comes to the aid of another person in the group, for example, 'I think what he was trying to say was . . .' or, 'She didn't mean that, she meant . . .' Although the 'rescuer's' intervention might initially ease the tension in the group, the action they take actually serves to inhibit rather than help the person they are seeking to rescue. Once someone has been 'rescued' it often demands a high level of confidence and determination to challenge the rescuer. Although rescuers can appear to be defending people, they are often actually seeking to silence them to avoid conflict which might cause anxiety within the group. A healthier approach is to give space to someone to continue and develop what they are saying, rather than speaking on their behalf.

Splitting

Child (to Dad)   'Mum says I can watch the film if it's okay with you.'

       (to Mum)   'Dad says I can watch the film.'

Splitting behaviour is founded on the principle of 'divide and rule'. It may involve one individual contacting other group members outside the group meeting to recruit support and is usually quite manipulative. It usually results in divisions within the group, possibly with subgroups emerging. Splitting can happen when divisions become apparent and issues are raised which are obviously difficult, but not acknowledged as such. For example, in a group where some members are perceived by others to not do their fair share of the work, comments might be made which highlight this issue, without raising it explicitly.

Splitting can also refer to the way in which individuals split off one side of themselves because they are unable to deal with it, communicating for example that they are never angry but rather always considerate of others or that they help others with difficulties but never have any needs of their own.

Groupthink

'Groupthink' is a term coined by Irving Janis, and describes a dynamic in groups which occurs when 'too high a price is placed on the harmony and morale of the group, so that loyalty to the group's previous policies, or to the group consensus, overrides the conscience of each member' (Handy, 1993, p. 163).

Janis noted that very cohesive groups became blinkered, particularly in situations where they faced criticism, stress or opposition, and acted in ways that potentially contradicted the values and normal behaviour of the individuals concerned. He identified several symptoms of groupthink (Handy, 1993, pp. 163–4):

- over-optimism or invulnerability
- rationalizing away things that do not 'fit'
- turning a blind eye to immoral issues
- stereotyping critics or enemies
- exerting pressure on those who voice doubts
- self-censorship – not allowing things to be discussed outside the group
- unanimity, or screening out other views
- mind-guards, who protect the decision.

With their desire to encourage unity, churches can inadvertently encourage a groupthink dynamic or mentality. Those who criticize or disagree can be labelled as dissenters or seen as rebellious. Disagreement or struggles with leadership can be rationalized as 'enemy attack'. Janis also identified ways to minimize groupthink (Janis, 1972, pp. 209–15) and these are helpful in preventing groups from falling into this way of working.

- Encourage group members to be 'critical evaluators' and to express objections or doubts.
- Those with authority should not express opinions when giving groups tasks.
- Encourage independent groups to work on the same issues.
- Examine and consider all possible effective alternatives.
- Give group members freedom to discuss ideas with trustworthy people outside the group.
- Invite outside experts to meetings so group members can discuss and question with them.
- Encourage different group members to take turns in playing 'devil's advocate'.

Identification

> When a person fully identifies with someone else, they lose the distinction between themselves and the other. When we cry in movies it is us who is crying, but that crying occurs because we experience emotions that are being expressed by someone else (or the image of someone else). We identify with the person who is crying and act as if that person is us. (Ringer, 2002, p. 136)

Identification in groups can affect the responses of individual group members significantly. For example, one individual may hear the group leader say something harsh or critical to another group member. The first person may identify with the person who has been harshly spoken to and might feel what they imagine that person to be feeling. On the basis of this they may then respond angrily or sharply to the group leader.

Projection

> Projection . . . occurs when we unconsciously cannot tolerate aspects of ourselves. In this case we disown what we do not like by failing to see those aspects in ourselves but projecting the disowned part of ourselves onto others and therefore seeing these characteristics in others. (Ringer, 2002, p. 133)

In groups, projection can result in people being labelled or scape-goated, or in them getting pushed into adopting certain roles. Projection can work on an individual level but we might also see 'mutual projection' which can result in the unofficial allocation of roles to particular group members. For example, a quieter group member might become identified as the 'sensitive' person. The rest of the group then respond as if this person is sensitive, not allowing them to inter-act normally with everyone else. This can be incredibly frustrating and usually results in further anxiety, which then increases the problem. Normally for projection to stick, there will be some kind of 'hook' – an area of weakness or vulnerability – in the person receiving it, but this dynamic can be very destructive for individuals and for the health of the whole group.

Analysing and responding to group processes

It has been suggested that interpretations of group behaviour are 25 per cent right 25 per cent of the time (Jaques, 1991, p. 4). This may be a little pessimistic but it emphasizes the imprecise nature of group processes and dynamics. Particularly with unconscious processes like groupthink, identification and projection, much experience and wisdom is needed if we are to address these effectively. One of the most positive ways of ensuring a healthy group dynamic is to develop and employ excellent facilitation skills. This will be addressed in the next chapter.

Points for reflection, discussion and action

- Think about groups that you have been part of. What norms and roles can you recognize?
- Where do you think groups you belong to currently are in their stage of development?
- What roles do you tend to adopt in groups?
- Where can you observe group dynamics at work in your church or organization? How do these affect work and relationships?
- As a leader what behaviour do you find most difficult? Has this chapter helped you identify why?

3

Facilitation skills

Good facilitation means doing less and being more.   (Lao Tzu)

We have already noted that if our understanding of collaborative ministry values the co-creation of ministry it will need collaborative leadership styles. There will inevitably be occasions where decisiveness and authority will be required but, in terms of overall style, we believe facilitative approaches will generally be most appropriate and effective. Discussions with students about what they would look for in a small group leader led Mallison to conclude that the most important three qualities would be love for Jesus, love for people and love for Christ's Church (1996, p. 46).

If love underpins our ministry, then our leadership approaches will seek to express this tangibly. The word facilitate originates from the Latin, literally 'to make easy', and describes a style of working with groups that is participative, process-focused, relational, empowering and focused on the group's needs. Facilitators are a resource to the processes – whether these involve learning, decision-making, pastoral care – rather than directive or didactic leaders or teachers. Although facilitation skills include classic leadership and teaching skills, which will come into play at specific times, the facilitative role is a 'helping' one which encourages group members to take responsibility and values their experience.

In learning contexts there is evidence that creativity is encouraged when facilitators don't dominate, that most participants prefer participatory approaches and that pleasant social relationships are most likely to develop in such contexts (Rogers, 1971, p. 85). This is equally important in ministry, where participation, creative thinking and good relationships are likely to significantly enhance the experience of collaborative working.

Self-awareness

> Growing your own style as a facilitator of groups means paying close
> attention to the complex constellation of feeling, thinking, action,
> intuition and memories and fantasies that is *you*. It means address-
> ing and dealing with your own vulnerability and failings.
>
> (Ringer, 2002, p. 19)

One of the most important things we bring to facilitation processes
is ourselves. Our values, attitudes, skills, personality and style will
have a significant impact – whether positively or negatively – on
the groups we facilitate. Self-awareness is crucial to ensure that our
influence is positive rather than damaging. 'Self-awareness involves
understanding our characteristic responses to situations so that we
can build on our positive qualities and be wary of any negative ones'
(Thompson, 1996, p. 9). We also need to be aware of our own needs
and how they are being met, to ensure that we do not manipulate
groups we are working with into meeting our needs for us.

Brian and Sarah had led a day's training for those involved in
preaching. As a final exercise, Sarah did an evaluation to get participant feedback. She divided the day into sections and asked
people to comment on each one. When it came to the section Brian
had led, he interrupted before anyone could speak. 'I felt really
intimidated. I bet you all thought I was rubbish compared to Sarah.'
Unsurprisingly, the participants' feedback form was overwhelmingly
positive, but it was impossible to tell what they really thought. Brian
was looking to the group for affirmation, but in a way that under-
mined the evaluation process and skewed the participants' responses.

We need to be aware of our own emotional responses and find
appropriate ways of getting our needs met. This might involve being
honest with the group and saying something like, 'I am feeling concerned that you are very quiet. I'd find it useful to know if what I'm
doing is helpful.' Here, the facilitator acknowledges the anxiety they
feel, but leaves space for honesty.

In many cases it will be most appropriate to meet our needs
outside the group context if we are to facilitate effectively, but we
must ensure that we do not neglect or undervalue these needs and
that we create space for reflection, support and encouragement for
ourselves. Some other important things to consider when it comes
to self-awareness:

- our strengths and where we might become overconfident;
- areas of weakness in skill or understanding;
- ability to take responsibility for our own values, beliefs and assumptions;
- vulnerable areas which might be triggers to upset or anger us or which might cause defensive reactions;
- integrity or congruence between what we say and who we are/how we live.

Issues of power in facilitation

As facilitators we will find ourselves using power in different ways at different times. Power may come as a result of our position or role (church leader, youth worker, home group leader, worship leader, trustee), the resources we might have at our disposal (money, status, privilege), our knowledge or expertise (qualifications, experience) or our personality (charisma, charm). To work or minister effectively, we will need to understand the power that we have and exercise it sensitively and appropriately.

If, as Handy argues, 'power and influence make up the fine texture of organizations, and indeed of all interactions' (Handy, 1993, p. 123), we cannot afford to be ignorant about power and our own relationship with it. In facilitation, appropriate use of power will enable us to be decisive and also to empower others, encouraging their participation. Using power inappropriately will inhibit participation and may significantly undermine our aims.

The home group leaders' meeting had started well with coffee, biscuits and chat. The group hadn't met together before but Karen the curate had felt for a long time that it would be helpful to do so. She had finally persuaded David, the vicar, to gather those leading home groups to chat, share ideas and discuss possibilities around the new parish plan. She tried carefully to create a participative environment and started by inviting people to share their encouraging news, and any views, questions and any concerns they had. She was heartened when a quiet woman in her fifties began to share a concern expressed by someone in her group about Sunday services. 'She just feels there isn't really anything for young families ...'

Before she could continue, David interrupted defensively, 'We really need you, as leaders to be supportive, not undermining the church leadership at this important time. I'm really surprised at your critical attitude, Mary.'

The room fell silent. Karen tried to continue the conversation but everyone appeared reluctant to contribute. David took the opportunity to share his ideas about the parish plan with the group. Apparently unaware of the impact of his intervention, he commented to Karen afterwards how positive he thought the meeting had been.

Autonomy

In working with adults in both church and learning contexts, one of our values is to encourage autonomy – or self-direction. Brookfield claims that adults desire self-directedness (1986, p. 63) and while we would not wish to challenge this, experience suggests that because of their personal constructs and prior experiences, many adults expect to be directed clearly and can struggle with issues of autonomy in many contexts. In some churches people are almost deskilled, as they are encouraged to be passive consumers of ministry and the organizational culture which emerges fosters dependence rather than autonomy.

To facilitate effectively, we need to create a culture which encourages autonomy. This might include:

- being open about wanting to see people owning their own processes and journey;
- encouraging people to set personal objectives;
- creating an atmosphere where questioning is valued;
- interactive, participative and empowering methodologies;
- encouraging the sharing of experience and skills from all present;
- negotiation about process;
- opportunities for individual reflection and interaction with the facilitator;
- minimizing facilitator power and empowering the group.

Culture-setting

We have already highlighted the ways in which culture can shape values, expectations and behaviour within groups. In a collaborative ministry context we should be aware of the power we have in creating a healthy culture in terms of the physical, emotional, relational and spiritual environment.

Physical environment

The current interest in DIY, garden design and interiors highlights how aware people are becoming of the significance of physical space, but in some contexts this is given little consideration. Those in churches may spend time thinking about the worship space and how that feels, but many church meetings we have attended have been held in settings which were in no way conducive to the task at hand.

Some issues around physical surroundings may seem to have little relevance to collaborative ministry but the extent to which people feel relaxed and comfortable in their physical space will affect their sense of being valued and being able to focus on the task. Anyone who has sat on uncomfortable chairs on a wintry evening in a cold church hall, with the lighting buzzing and flickering, will be aware of how distracting an uncomfortable physical environment can be. In seeking to create surroundings conducive to a positive collaborative experience we might want to consider the following issues.

Assess the purpose and appropriateness of the space for the task. If we are having a focused time of discussion and planning it may be better to avoid meeting somewhere where members of the group will be distracted by family commitments or the telephone. Meeting in homes may help with babysitting issues, but can be a distraction as well as a blessing for the person concerned. It may sometimes be more helpful to help find a good babysitter and arrange to meet for a shorter time somewhere more conducive.

The group size affects the amount of space needed. Rooms should be big enough not to feel cramped, but not so large that a small group rattles around. Physical proximity increases interaction. If the room is overlarge, seek to create a smaller, designated area through the positioning of chairs, furniture, plants or screens. Consider issues of light and heat, ensuring that both are adequate and suitable.

Aesthetic issues are also important. Beautiful surroundings are not important to everyone, but simple things can make a difference to a room's atmosphere. Enhance the space by ensuring that it is clean and tidy and using furniture, flowers, fruit and plants where possible.

Check visibility, particularly where visual aids are to be used, sound (Is amplification needed for a bigger group? Will traffic or other noise be a distraction?) and accessibility. This is an issue not only for disabled people, but also in terms of how easy it is for participants to find. Basic things like the proximity and number of toilets and other facilities should also be taken into consideration, and borne in mind when planning comfort breaks.

Think about the types and positioning of seating. In a small group or team meeting people should be able to see one another and communicate effectively. Think too about what seating positions communicate about power within the group. A circle is more empowering and encourages greater participation than a group of chairs facing a 'leader'. One person standing while others sit immediately shifts the balance of power and makes participation more difficult. Physical boundaries (tables, desks, a lectern) can prevent groups forming effectively (Handy, 1993, p. 170).

Emotional and relational environment

The emotional climate created within the session is as important as the physical. Facilitators can do much to create an atmosphere which maximizes participation and ownership and minimizes anxiety for those involved. Setting the emotional climate within a group is one of the facilitator's key responsibilities. First, we should approach the group with the right attitude and underlying values. Tough (in Brookfield, 1986, p. 63) says that ideal helpers:

- are warm, loving, caring and accepting;
- have high regard for the competence of those they work with;
- view learning experiences as dialogue;
- are open to change and seeking to learn themselves.

These characteristics may help us reflect on the kind of facilitators we may wish to be. It is also essential to recognize that everyone's experience of the group will be different.

Rapport

Seeking to develop relationships at the beginning of a session can make a real difference to participants' experience. This can be done through welcoming, eye contact and by maintaining a relaxed, friendly, warm and non-threatening attitude. Those of us with responsibility must not be so preoccupied with 'task' issues that we fail to engage effectively and relationally with the group. Preparations of the venue should be done earlier or delegated to allow time for welcoming and conversation. Having drinks or nibbles available can be really valuable in creating a relaxed environment. Those in more 'full-time' ministry can often forget that someone who works long hours and has had to travel from work may arrive for an evening meeting having not had time to eat beforehand – a cup of coffee and a couple of (good quality!) biscuits can make all the difference. Icebreakers or clear introductions can help group rapport develop at the beginning of a session, but these should be appropriate to the group and not leave those involved too vulnerable (for more see pp. 19–20). Simple questions are more appropriate than embarrassing or complex activities.

Boundary-setting

Setting clear boundaries so that the group knows what to expect helps to create a secure and safe space in which people feel they can participate. We have already talked about the process of group contracts (see p. 19) and these can be referred back to later by the facilitator or by members of the group if the boundaries are not respected.

As facilitators, being explicit about our expectations can provide freedom for the group. We may be quite happy for people to interrupt, ask questions, get up and walk around and go to the toilet whenever they wish but, unless we communicate this, group members may feel inhibited. Being clear about the freedoms people have can help create a relaxed and informal atmosphere. It may be necessary to 'model' permission-giving, if a group is unused to informal settings. For example, during our training sessions we often encourage adult learners to help themselves to drinks whenever they wish. Sometimes they may be reluctant to do this because of their experiences of more formal learning environments, so we will often take the first opportunity available to pour a drink – for example, when they are doing an activity in small groups.

Language

Awareness of language and assumptions is also an important aspect of culture-setting. Using long words or jargon can intimidate some people and make them reluctant to participate. Being aware that language can liberate or oppress is important in facilitation. Ensuring that the first opportunities to contribute to discussion give most people an opportunity to share an experience can break the ice and increase confidence.

Clarifying purpose

We need to be explicit about the group's agenda and purpose. Even if we feel people know why they are there it is worth revisiting both purpose and aims to ensure clarity. Agendas are useful here – but need to be realistic. Presenting people with an unachievable list is detrimental to morale. Part of the facilitator's role is to keep people 'to task' and to ensure the group stays focused. Getting the balance right here can be a challenge.

Spiritual environment

Finally, it is important to consider the spiritual climate and environment we are seeking to create. Ensuring that God is the centre and focus of our activities may appear self-evident, but needs thought and planning. In busy meetings prayer can often be sidelined. Starting with silence, reflection or prayer can help to focus the group and can give individuals opportunity to centre themselves from wherever they have come from.

Encouraging participation

This can sometimes be a challenge. Where organizations have a hierarchical style of leadership, adopting a facilitative approach may challenge the norms and culture of the group and individual expectations of group members. Particularly where there is a strong culture of dependency, this may at first feel quite threatening for group members. For some facilitators, issues around their own personality and ability to step out of the limelight may hinder a facilitative process (Rogers, 1971, p. 89). This can be a challenge for many in ministry, particularly those who have inherited models of ministry which are 'performance-oriented' or focused around a charismatic personality.

Leadership approaches which create a culture in which questioning is viewed as rebellion or undermining will often lead to those with responsibility having a warped and unrealistic view of their own role and how they are perceived by others. Where facilitators are hindered by a lack of objectivity about their role in the group (Rogers, 1971, p. 89), this can be helped by good self-awareness, clear understanding of group processes and an awareness of the interaction between the two. This demands wisdom, humility and a willingness to listen, encourage questioning and give and receive feedback.

We need to think carefully about how to practically encourage participation, particularly if a group is unused to this. Planned processes can be helpful and might include approaches like:

- breaking into small groups or pairs to discuss an issue before exploring it as a whole group – this gives opportunity for quieter group members to 'try out' their thoughts beforehand and prevents more confident members from dominating;
- using post-it notes or flip-chart paper for people to write or draw thoughts, ideas or contributions on.

Facilitating discussions

Discussions are likely to be central in collaborative ministry groups and can encourage participation effectively. Healthy discussion nurtures respectful and attentive listening, creates space for and encourages appreciation of different viewpoints and perspectives and allows exploration of issues and possibilities. Discussions can potentially engender collaborative learning together as well as ministering together.

> Discussion is one of the best ways to foster growth because it is premised on the idea that only through collaboration and cooperation with others can we be exposed to new points of view. This exposure increases our understanding and renews our motivation to continue learning. In the process our democratic instincts are confirmed: by giving the floor to as many different participants as possible, a collective wisdom emerges that would have been impossible for any of the participants to achieve on their own. (Brookfield and Preskill, 1999, p. 3)

Thinking about the facilitator's role in discussion, it is again important to be aware of power. Facilitators can sometimes dominate. This can be because of a fear of silence, but it is essential to give space for people to think before they respond and not to be afraid of quiet. We may need to reassure the group if there is anxiety about this, or give structured silent times, 'Why don't we just spend a few moments in silence thinking about this . . .' Sometimes facilitators may undervalue or underestimate what others have to offer, place too much value on their own opinions or come with a pre-planned personal agenda. It is easy in preparing a meeting, a Bible study or a planning group to consider everything we want to say beforehand, but this can prevent us from listening effectively to others. At times facilitators who also hold a leadership position may feel they need to intervene to correct group members or give the 'party line' on an issue. However tempting this may be, caution should be exercised as it can significantly change the group dynamic.

If we are aware of a tendency to dominate or talk too much, it may help to practise using different types of question. As long as we give space for the group to respond, asking questions can encourage participation usefully. We may be familiar with using closed questions, requiring a 'yes' or 'no' answer, or open questions, which leave space for a fuller response, but other types of question can be equally useful in discussions:

- clarifying questions, to check understanding and invite further thinking: 'So do you mean . . . ?', 'Are you saying . . . ?'
- questions which raise awareness or encourage thinking about something that has happened, people's feelings and responses
- questions which invite elaboration: 'Can you say more about . . . ?'
- hypothetical questions, to stretch thinking or apply ideas to different situations: 'What if . . . ?', 'How might that work if . . . ?'
- questions that probe beyond the surface of an issue.

Some types of questions will be unhelpful. Where possible we should avoid multiple questions, loaded or leading questions, trick questions and long-winded questions.

Reluctance to contribute

Squirrell (1998, p. 85) suggests several reasons why people might not contribute and stay largely silent within a group:

- personal problems
- fear of looking stupid or failing
- lack of interest

- depression
- effects of medication
- problems with other group members
- lack of confidence or feelings of intimidation.

As facilitators we may need to assist people to participate and break silence. Direct appeals through inviting specific contributions can work, particularly if we know the silent member of the group has knowledge or expertise which will enable them to give helpful input. It may be that an individual has a reflective learning style and needs more time to think and consider before contributing to discussions. Allowing thinking time before inviting comment can sometimes be beneficial here.

Collaborative facilitation

There are huge advantages to co-facilitation. In planning, confidence and creativity can be engendered as ideas are shared and sessions structured. In the group itself it can be incredibly advantageous to have one person observing while someone else facilitates and then swapping over. When done well, co-facilitation can create a vibrant dynamic within the group as well as modelling collaborative approaches, different ways of working and perhaps different views and opinions.

In collaborative facilitation, preparation is as important as the face-to-face work with the group. Our experience is that, possibly because of time pressures, attention tends to be focused on the task aspects of the planning – what will be done within the group – rather than on thinking through issues of values and process. However, it is vitally important to explore carefully with co-facilitators our values in working with groups, our aims and objectives for the task, our expectations of the group and one another and if and how we wish our co-facilitator to intervene should difficulties arise. Brown highlights how significant issues can often be missed in these explorations:

> Fundamental attributes like age, gender, disability and race, often get played down in the choice of co-worker and omitted from their discussions of the co-worker relationship. Yet . . . these fundamental characteristics of the workers will have a profound affect on the members, who are likely to bring to the group stereotypical assumptions about

for example who holds the power in male/female and black/white relationships. In addition to the impact on the members, both co-workers are likely to have strong feelings about whether their partner is of the same or a different age, sex and ethnicity which will affect how they work together, particularly if these feelings are not voiced.

(Brown, 1994, p. 83)

Our experiences of co-facilitating with our spouses and with others have shown that good awareness of the other person's values, personality and approaches is essential in working together. Issues of power need to be clarified and any sense of competitiveness eradicated if the experience is to work.

Co-working means sharing the responsibility for work in the group fairly evenly, with neither partner consistently dominating or deferring to the other. There needs to be a sensitivity to what your colleague is feeling, experiencing and thinking, and an ability to support but not to over-protect when facing difficulties.   (Brown, 1994, p. 86)

We also should be aware that certain group dynamics – like splitting – are more likely to emerge in a co-facilitated group, as members 'play off' facilitators against each other. It can be healthy for groups to see that facilitators have different opinions on issues, but we need wisdom in this – modelling respect for difference sets a better example and creates a better atmosphere than argument and petty 'point scoring'. In this respect co-facilitators need to be secure within themselves and also with the person they are working with.

Before the session, Jo felt that she and Reg had communicated well. They had discussed the material to be covered, what his involvement would be and clarified aims. They had used a co-facilitation agreement to explore expectations, potential problems and values, though Reg asked to take this away rather than fill it in together. He said he would return it but never did. Some points needed clarifying, and this was done by telephone. During the session though, Reg did not cover the content agreed, he didn't participate as a member of the group but sat and watched as an observer and he used a style which was more akin to lecturing than the participative approaches they had agreed on.

Although Jo felt adequate time had been set aside to talk to Reg, she had overestimated the quality of the communication that had taken place. She had also overestimated Reg's understanding and the level at which he was listening. She should have asked him to clarify what he had understood from their conversations and insisted on working through the co-facilitation agreement together, even though that might have been hard work. In retrospect Jo recognized that she was intimidated because he was older, but realized afterwards that Reg had actually felt intimidated by her. Because of her assumptions about him she hadn't given him the encouragement, boundaries and affirmation she would have done if she had been working with someone younger.

A biblical perspective

Effective facilitators will have a developed understanding of processes and an excellent set of practical skills, but facilitation at its best is more than this. In many ways it is more an art than a science and, reflecting on the nature of the facilitator's role, it is helpful to consider the Holy Spirit as a metaphor. The Johannine description of the Spirit as Paraclete – 'one who comes alongside' (Vine, 1985, p. 208) – is particularly apt. The Spirit speaks (1 Timothy 4.1), opens understanding (1 Corinthians 2.12), leads into truth (1 John 2.27), teaches (John 16.13), enables (John 4.24) and empowers (Acts 1.8). The Spirit does not however override the free will of the individual, who can choose to resist, quench, grieve or respond to the Spirit (Pimlott, 2005).

The Spirit's role in the new birth of believers points us to another metaphor – that of midwife. Socrates learned principles from his mother who was a midwife, which he then applied to his inductive method of dialoguing with students. He used 'maieutics' – ways of drawing out ideas latent in students' minds. This process of reflective practice, commonly referred to as 'Socratic midwifery', highlights the importance of dialogue, valuing experience and the use of questioning in facilitative processes. Three elements of the midwife's role can be seen as particularly relevant to facilitation.

The importance of 'being alongside' echoes the image of Spirit-as-paraclete: the term midwife in English is derived from 'with-woman', emphasizing the helping and supportive rather than controlling nature of the role.

The importance of wisdom: in many civilizations the midwife was (or is) known as the 'wise woman' (for example, in French *sage-femme*).

The kind of knowledge facilitators need is not simply about technique, but more akin to wisdom – an integrated understanding. The Bible's use of the Trinitarian 'wisdom, knowledge and understanding' (Proverbs 3.19–20; 24.3–4) is helpful here. This wisdom is akin to intuition, 'the soul voice speaking' (Estés, 1992, p. 85) – a quality which is to some extent innate, but can be learned and developed.

The importance of mystery: in addition to the technical demands of the midwife's role, there is traditionally a 'mystical' aspect. In primitive societies, where women had no access to education, midwives were widely believed to have mystical or magical powers. A sense of mystery is significant in understanding facilitation and one reason why the metaphor of the Spirit appears so relevant. As John 3 emphasizes, the ways of the Spirit are not easily defined or explained. Facilitation skills can be learned, developed and improved, but there is a mystery at the heart of the process, which makes it both challenging and exciting. However experienced we become, we can never accurately predict the outcome of each different context. The complex mixture of factors involved in the dynamics of working with individuals and groups contain elements which cannot easily be organized, understood or controlled.

'Our world is populated with domesticated grownups, who would rather settle for safe, predictable answers instead of wild, unpredictable mystery' (Yaconelli, 1998, p. 166). To embrace this kind of mystery is to rediscover a childlike attitude to learning, living and growing. It will encourage us to acknowledge those areas in which we are weak, at the same time growing our awareness of the skills we do have and the incredible potential within ourselves and others to discover and push back boundaries. Effective facilitators draw from a deep inner resource of skills, values, knowledge, experience and personal qualities, which enables them to face whatever arises within the groups they are working with without being overwhelmed or intimidated.

Points for reflection, discussion and action

- What do you believe to be your strengths and weaknesses in terms of your own self-awareness? How could you develop this further?
- In what ways could you seek to create positive environments in the contexts you work in?

- In which situations might it be helpful to be more aware of the power you exercise?
- How could you increase participation within groups you facilitate?
- How do you feel about co-facilitation in a collaborative ministry context? Reflect on your experiences in this area, any positives you can see and any concerns you might have.

4

Reflecting skills

Joyce Rupp (1996, p. 56) talks about 'a journey without maps', which is an excellent analogy for ministry. We don't always know what is going to happen, where we are going or why things occur but reflecting skills help us to make sense of our experiences. Van der Ven (1998, p. 86) highlights the problem people in ministry face: 'because of the complexity and inherent dynamic of the situation in which the pastor is involved, every solution generates its own problem or even problems.' Ben, an experienced schools worker, had a reflective practice 'moment' when a 19-year-old female member of the team took her first assembly. Her input was not as proficient as his, but her age and the fact that she had gone to the school in question meant that she had the total and undivided attention of the pupils. Ben discovered that his age, ability and skill were not the most significant factors in his work. As a result of this reflection he then set about a two-year process of stopping doing such work and passing it onto younger people. In collaborative ministry there will be many such incidents that we can learn from and that result in changed practice.

In the caring professions, reflecting skills, often known as reflective practice, is a core part of initial training and ongoing development. Moon suggests that reflection is one of our basic mental processes and that it is most often used where there is not an obvious solution or material is ill-structured or uncertain (2000, p. 10). Both general reflecting and theological reflection skills are useful in collaborative ministry. Both are about developing, interpreting, improving and assessing our practice with the aim of drawing conclusions which lead to a change in thinking, action, attitude or new insights or approaches. Reflection should make a difference; the word sounds passive but it leads to action. Reflecting is useful for a range of purposes including learning from experience, making decisions, exploring problems, developing theory or practice principles, justifying decisions to stakeholders, integrating values into practice, self-development or team-building.

Reflection should be seen as a spiral, we sometimes use a toy slinky to illustrate this. You never begin your next piece of reflection where you started the last as reflection should move you on in some way each time you do it.

What is reflective practice?

Reflective practice is 'an approach to professional practice that emphasises the need for practitioners to avoid standardised, formula responses to the situations they encounter' (Thompson, 1996, p. 221). Reflective practice is a discipline, it is an activity that if practised often enough becomes habitual, it becomes integrated into what we do and who we are. In ministry there are rarely situations where we can do what we did last time; it requires us to reflect and work out an appropriate response.

A Muslim woman knocked on Paul's chaplaincy office door, clearly in distress; her son was on the intensive care unit. She did not ask to see a Muslim chaplain and asked Paul for religious instruction to sustain her at this difficult time. This is not a normal experience for Paul. He was not sure what he was most thrown by, the fact a female Muslim was speaking alone with him by choice in his office or that she was asking for spiritual help from a Christian, or that he had no idea of what to say to her. Not wanting to offend, he started with some Old Testament prophets as this would hopefully find some common ground. His knowledge of Islam at that time was limited and she listened to his inadequate wanderings. Not knowing what else to say he finally and very tentatively said that what he used with some Christian families was the 'Footprints' poem and would she like him to read it to her. He was unsure of what she would make of a Christian poem, but thought that prefacing it with 'Christian' would at least give a get-out clause if it did not connect with her or was offensive. He read it and immediately her eyes lit up and her spirit lifted. She said that it was very interesting that he had read this poem to her as the day before her teenage son had been taken ill, his uncle had given him a copy of the 'Footprints' poster to put up on his wall. His mind began again to whirr. How could this be? Were they seeking out Christianity? Had a Christian given it to them? No, he soon realized as he reflected on the words of the poem, which he must have read scores of times. It did not mention Jesus but God and there was nothing in this poem that was uniquely Christian. He gave her a copy of the card and they went on to the ward to visit her son, as she had then asked Paul to come and pray for him! This experience and reflection although surprising and shocking at the time resulted in a paradigm shift when he realized how easy it is to read Christological or Trinitarian models into something; we make assumptions that are not always based on reality.

Johns (2004, p. 2) uses the term 'layers of reflection' and identifies five stages that move from doing reflection to reflection as a way of being:

1 *Reflection-on-experience* Reflecting on a situation or experience after the event with the intention of drawing insights that may inform future practice in positive ways.
2 *Reflection-in-action* Pausing within a particular situation or experience in order to make sense and reframe the situation proceeding towards desired outcomes.
3 *The internal supervisor* Dialoguing with self while in conversation with another in order to make sense.
4 *Reflection-within-the-moment* Being aware of the way I am thinking, feeling and responding within the unfolding moment and dialoguing with self to ensure I am interpreting and responding congruently to whatever is unfolding. It is having some space in your mind to change your ideas rather than being fixed to certain ideas.
5 *Mindful practice* Being aware of self within the unfolding moment with the intention of realizing desirable practice (however desirable is defined).

It would be interesting to work on this as a collaborative ministry team so that reflection becomes integral to the way that we work. The tools in the final part of this chapter introduce some ways of approaching reflection methodically and activities suggested in some of the other chapters also encourage reflective approaches.

Reflection can bring rich insights. At meetings of the Grove Youth Series Editorial Group <www.grovebooks.co.uk> the day begins with a reflection, which may be based around a story, an experience, an object, a picture, and often each person present shares their insights. The sum of our reflections is much more enriching than just listening to one person and it highlights new perspectives, different interpretations and fresh ways of seeing something. This is helpful in getting us into a creative, reflective way of thinking at the beginning of a meeting.

Reflective practice processes and tools

This is a basic framework for reflective practice which lists the steps we need to go through:

1 *Name* What is the situation/issue/dilemma/problem/question?
2 *Explore* What do we hope will emerge from this reflective practice process?
  What is the end result/product/consequence . . . that we are looking for?
3 *Analyse* What is/could be going on?
  Have we made any assumptions or presuppositions?
  How do we/others think/feel?
  What would our values, motives, goals, agenda, purpose, tradition, discipline want to say?
  What theory or previous experience informs this?
  We can also add faith, the Bible, theology, Christian tradition and culture here as tools for analysis.
4 *Evaluate* What were/are our options?
  What would we change/do differently?
  What are the possibilities?
  What are the strengths and weaknesses of these?
  Why did we come to this conclusion/do this . . . ?
  Again we can draw in faith resources at this stage.
5 *Outcome* What is the outcome of this process?
  New learning, different practice, action, insight . . .

Critical incident technique

A succinct version of this is offered by Thompson (2006, p. 55) who has a four-stage process:

1 identifying an incident that has caused concern;
2 clarifying what happened in that incident;

3 seeking an explanation for what happened;
4 looking for alternative explanations.

Gibbs' reflective cycle

Gibbs offers another process in what he calls a 'reflective cycle' (cited in Moon, 2000, p. 73):

1 *Description* What happened?
2 *Feelings* What were you thinking and feeling?
3 *Evaluation* What was good and bad?
4 *Analysis* What sense can you make of the situation?
5 *Conclusion* What else could you have done?
6 *Action plan* If it occurs again, what would you do?

Generating options and possibilities

Brainstorming is a core activity in reflection where you identify as many answers as possible to a question or reasons for a behaviour or solutions to a problem, etc. Trying to do this by seeing things from a different perspective can be helpful, for example, from the standpoint of someone else who is not represented in the reflection group, or from five years in the future.

Issue-based questions

If you want to focus on a specific issue then generate a list of questions to explore. This is one we use with youth workers on power.

• Consider a situation/incident/event, e.g. a pastoral encounter, an argument in the youth group over use of the pool table, a discussion at the deacons' meeting over some damage done in the church hall, a discussion on how we are going to celebrate our centenary, responding to a request at the PCC from a yoga teacher to use church for classes, etc.
• Where is/was the power?
• Who has the power?
• Who was disempowered?
• Who was disempowering?
• Who did not have power?
• Who would like power?
• Who did/might abuse power?

- Who needs power?
- What is power in this context?

Paul often uses reflective practice tools in his work as a chaplain. Gregory came to see Paul because a job had been offered him after only a year in his current post; this was a dilemma. Together they explored the frustrations that Gregory was experiencing in his current job and the attractiveness of a way out. However, at the analysis stage Gregory realized that this new job would not be the easy answer he thought as he recognized that it would mean a lot of management and administration when his passion was face-to-face work. In evaluating his options he realized that it would be a case of out of the frying pan into the fire and he decided to stay. However, the offer had unsettled him and he became aware that he had made a mistake taking his current job and resolved to look for one which was a better match to his calling and gifting.

Having 'stop and think' times in our practice to develop what we do is valuable; we would almost say essential. Designating times for this to happen works well as does appointing a facilitator to encourage and aid the reflection. Working on real-life situations helps us develop skills and understanding for when we face other complex situations in the future and helps us integrate new learning.

Theological reflection

Theological reflection is related to reflective practice; it uses the same or very similar processes but additionally engages with our faith at every stage. We could describe it as being like a child with one parent who brings professional knowledge and expertise and the other who brings theological skills. Which one has the most influence depends on us!

Theological reflection involves asking where God is in this situation or experience and making connections with Christian tradition, theology, the Bible, our faith and experiences of ministry. It is about the God we find, not the God we bring. It assumes God and the principles of the kingdom are already present; it becomes our task to discern where and how. Theological reflection should lead to the integration of new knowledge or understanding into our practice, attitudes, frames of reference, etc. The process can be significant:

'Theological reflection changes lives. The practice of theological reflection helps us take religious insights, which are fleeting, and gradually move them into our permanent structures of perceiving and interpreting experience' (Killen and De Beer, 1994, p. 111). In asking our students how they benefit from reflecting theologically we get a range of responses. It:

• helps me gain a bigger picture and brings a wholeness to my practice; it brings practice and theology into partnership;
• gives me models for practice, e.g. incarnation, liberation;
• helps me to stop and think about my practice and ways in which I can move forward, helps evaluate strategies, brings personal and professional development and motivation;
• helps me not to compromise my Christian principles and brings consistency between life and practice – integrity; helps keep me humble and open to learning from others;
• challenges perceived ideas, preconceptions and helps me identify root motives and issues;
• gives me confidence, empowers me through exploring the 'why' of what I am doing;
• bonds workers together if done corporately;
• gives me a greater awareness of God and the seeking of God in everyday situations, to understand God's guidance and keep God at the centre of my youth work.

Key questions to move from reflective practice to theological reflection

Classically, theological reflection gives primary authority to experience although some people will prefer to reflect starting from the Bible or theology. These reflections encompass:

• What within our faith resources helps us make sense of, resonates with, surprises, challenges, is reflected in, speaks to, listens to, critiques this situation/issue, etc.?
• What within this situation/issue helps us make sense of, resonates with, surprises, challenges, is reflected in, speaks to, listens to, critiques our faith, mission, ministry, actions, attitudes, understanding, calling, thinking, etc.?

What do you reflect on?

The simple answer is anything, 'The mundane and the joyous moments serve just as well as occasions upon which we may reflect and learn to think theologically' (De Bary, 2003, p. 121). For example, as a youth worker we may have gone into a school, are walking along the corridor with the deputy head and suddenly one of our youth group comes up to us and gives us a hug and kiss. How do we avoid this happening again? Or we may have noticed that numbers are dropping off at the luncheon club or that we seem to have lost a little of our joy for the everyday tasks of our job or there seem to be tensions in the team but we can't quite pinpoint why.

When to reflect?

When most of us think about reflection, we think about an activity that takes place after an event. Schon (1991) talks about reflection before, during and after an event. During the annual carols by candlelight, which is the most important service of the year for the local community, one person in the team is asked to make notes as to what is working, is too long, has gone well, etc. When the team debrief the event they use these notes alongside others' recollections from the service. Being purposeful about reflection can be helpful as before an event we can be caught up with all the finer details of organization and after an event it can just not happen at all as we move on to the next pressing commitment. A more formal evaluation process as described in Chapter 10 may be helpful in this sort of instance. Sometimes it is a fine line as to whether you call something reflective practice or evaluation.

Theological reflection process

This is a simple three-stage process Paul developed from the classic see, judge, act model. This resulted from a piece of reflective practice in realizing that the word 'judge' is interpreted negatively by many, particularly in a youth work context. It also adds a range of resources or perspectives that you may want to reflect on or from. At each stage we choose one or two words to work with that resonate with us.

Observe, assess, respond

For each of the three phases, choose one or more of the key words that most resonate with the topic, issue, situation, dilemma, etc. that you are exploring, e.g. what sort of observing were you engaging in? The lists under 'Consider' give you a wide range of contexts that you need to think about in relation to the reflection; choose the ones that are pertinent to you.

Observe

Where, when, who, how, why, what are you observing?

This stage encourages us to really get under the skin of what we are reflecting on, to ask again and again, What is or could be going on?

Purpose and key words Detect, investigate, insight, imagine, scrutinize, perceive, examine, witness, explore, discover, probe, glimpse, discriminate, discern, become aware of . . .

Consider Situation, dynamics, agendas, expectations, fears, hopes, human development, group theory, pressures, personality, gender, ethnicity, class, disability, culture, state of mind, health education, atmosphere, environment, weather, motives . . .

Assess

What, why, when, where and how are you assessing?

This stage is where we have a conversation between our experience and ministerial and theological resources and work to a conclusion.

Purpose and key words Mediate, arbitrate, adjudicate, critique, decide, judge, conclude, ascertain, determine, consider, pronounce, realize, review, evaluate . . .

Consider Past experience, church tradition, theology, Bible, metaphors, theory, power, history, ministerial principles, professionalism, social and political context, culture, subculture . . .

Respond

Where, when, how and why should you respond?

This last stage is all about outcome. In the light of the conclusions of the previous stages, what have we learnt or would do differently next time?

Purpose and key words Do something, proceed, be active, act, react, change, take action, start, move towards, learn, initiate, develop, begin, instigate, initiate, plan, think differently . . .

Consider Restrictions, expectations, hopes, need, resources, desires, short/medium/long-term plans, vision, reactions, consequences . . .

This process can be used to reflect on almost anything. The more tools we access from our Christian faith the richer and more rounded our reflection will be and we need to ensure we progress to an outcome.

An example of collaborative theological reflection happened when the three of us were on an away day to reflect on our work with the Midlands Centre for Youth Ministry. We reflected on the degree course in youth and community work and applied theology that we run and noted that we have put a lot of energy into ensuring that students meet the competences needed to gain a professional qualification in youth work but had not articulated as clearly the ministerial formation of our students. We explored a metaphor of streams and in talking and reflecting together a concept emerged of holistic learning and formation where we focus on five streams: professional, ministerial, personal, spirituality and academic. Everyone involved in the course now gets a bookmark which has both the words and a picture of interwoven strands.

To conclude a collaboratively taught module on ministry, Paul facilitates an exercise where students explore their values and calling, individually and corporately, as Christian youth workers. After a morning of preparation students displayed their work in the chapel and contributed to corporate posters on such issues as 'What does it mean to be a Christian youth worker?' or 'If Jesus was speaking to young people today, what would he say?' Finally, they together visit each person's work to discuss issues arising from what is presented. Ideas such as these are developed in *Tools for Reflective Ministry* (Paul Nash and Sally Nash, SPCK, 2009).

Issues around reflection

The way we reflect is partly dependent on who we are, our age, gender, ethnicity, personality, disability and other factors that shape our perceptions. Farley (2002, p. 17) illustrates the differences from the perspective of a theologian:

Even as a theologian is contextual by way of location and situation, even as such things as gender, ethnicity, nationality, language and economic system render the theologian biologically and culturally specific, so is the theologian contextual by way of participation in a community of faith.

When reflecting in a group some of this needs to be acknowledged as often conflict emerges because of our differences, which are not always identified as contributing to the conflict. Spelling out our preconceptions and assumptions as we begin to reflect together can help us understand each other and realize some of the inferences and roots of what people say. Sally, for example, reacts badly to non-inclusive language being used but doesn't always remember to suggest this as one of the ground rules.

Although there is not scope here to discuss this in detail, learning styles impact the way that we reflect and we need to try and ensure that the activities we use relate to people's preferences. Learning from reflection will be more effective if this is the case. Honey and Mumford (1992, pp. 5–6) describe people as activists, reflectors, theorists and pragmatists. Activists 'involve themselves fully and without bias in new experiences. They enjoy the here and now and are happy to be dominated by immediate experiences.' Reflectors 'like to stand back to ponder experiences and observe them from many different perspectives . . . and prefer to think about it thoroughly before coming to any conclusion'. Theorists 'adapt and integrate observations into complex but logically sound theories'. Pragmatists 'are keen on trying out ideas, theories and techniques to see if they work in practice. They positively search out new ideas and take the first opportunity to experiment with applications.' Many of the exercises and ideas in this book can be presented in a way that can facilitate participation from people of a variety of learning styles.

Reflection can happen by chance encounter as well as deliberate intention. Being willing to hear from those who do not usually have a voice can have powerful consequences. A pastoral care worker mentioned to the minister that one of the women from the parent and toddlers group she was seeing, who had recently had a miscarriage, was disappointed that the church did not have any sort of memorial service so that the event could be publicly marked. The leadership team considered the idea and invited another local church leader who had experience in this to come and talk to them.

They decided to go ahead with the project and much to their surprise had nearly 200 people at a service. This happened because they listened to someone on the fringe of the church.

If we work in a multidisciplinary collaborative context it is interesting to reflect on whether we should draw on theology in reflection if some of our partners are not Christians. Tanner (2002, p. 116) makes this challenge:

> Theology's warrant now centres on the question of whether theologians have anything important to say about the world and our place in it. What, if anything, can the Christian theologian positively contribute to the search for the true and the right on particular issues of importance in the twenty-first century?

In working with Christian students who want to do youth work in both faith-based and secular settings we are aware of a desire on the part of many not to have to leave their beliefs at home. Finding ways of helpfully introducing insights from our reflection that are theological or biblical in origin may often need to be part of the final stage where we determine what our response is and how we will enact it.

Reflecting in a group

Paul was sharing in a Communion service and was reflecting on a postcard of a stained-glass window from the prayer chapel at Buckfast Abbey in Devon. The window is about the size of the side of a two-storey house and shows Jesus, arms outstretched, behind a Communion table. Each time Paul prays in that chapel he hears Jesus say, 'Come' and this has had a profound impact on him. When Paul shared this thought with his fellow pilgrims, a woman in the group shared that this is not what she heard or felt at all, she heard, 'Go.' This obviously resonates with the biblical mandate of Matthew 28 to go into all the world and the cliché that we have a go-spel, not a come-spel. Paul still reflects on this many years after the event, acknowledging that he was both shocked and upset that the woman did not hear the same thing as he did from his special place. But the engagement with a wider group of people took him out of his comfort zone, and when he goes into the chapel now, he still hears 'Come' but also remembers that Jesus says, 'Go.'

Reflecting in a group helps us get a shared perspective on an issue and helps us to understand each other and hopefully work together more effectively. Having 'stop and think' times can be really valuable. A ministry team has an away day each year which explores some of the big picture and philosophical issues relating to their ministry. They have an external facilitator who encourages and aids reflection as well as asking questions that may not have been thought of. Honestly engaging in reflection requires a degree of vulnerability and will work best in teams where there is trust and the commitment to be collaborative. Taking it in turns to bring something to reflect on is helpful, ideally prepared beforehand, so the session has a focus and real-life situations are explored. In these sorts of circumstances new learning often emerges which can be integrated into existing knowledge and understanding.

Problem-solving

Theological reflection can help in problem-solving. One of the benefits of theologically reflecting in a group is that it gives an opportunity to deal with situations or problems that otherwise may not be dealt with properly or may continue to fester below the surface. Dom, a young person in Jack's youth group, said he was giving up his mechanics course at college. Jack spoke to Dom and sought to persuade him not to give up, he did not have long to go and soon he could get a job and earn some money. Dom decided not to go back to college and was still out of work and college a year later. Jack was troubled about how he and others had handled the situation but as he was not sure how to deal with this concern he decided to raise it at a team meeting as something to reflect on. The discussion led to exploring what 'shalom' meant for Dom and how they as youth workers needed to be trying to work towards that with him. They realized that they had taken his responses at face value and hadn't really tried to get to the bottom of what was happening or to engage him in working out what God was calling him to and supporting him in a journey to find that out. One of their aims as a church was to help people find 'life in all its fullness' (John 10.10) and the youth workers acknowledged they had let Dom down because none of them had got close enough for Dom to feel secure in sharing what the issues really were.

Theologically reflecting on this type of situation gives us the opportunity to engage positively and learn from an experience even if we felt we failed or didn't do all we could. This can be especially helpful to those of us who have a tendency to avoid conflict. Both the conflict and diversity chapters contain material that help take us forward in similar situations.

Theological perspectives

A word which is used in both the secular and biblical perspectives on reflection is 'wisdom'. Moon (2000, p. 9) identifies wisdom as a concept that encompasses higher-level reflective skills. Wisdom from this perspective includes an ability to cope with uncertain knowledge, understanding that knowledge is fallible, realizing the limitations of problem-solving strategies and the ability to make astute decisions. Wisdom in this understanding implies a relationship between knowing and action. There is also a body of wisdom literature within the Bible that may be helpful to explore in parallel with this as part of the desire to integrate both professional and biblical/theological insights. Proverbs encourages us to seek after wisdom and seeking God is a part of reflecting for those looking to integrate their faith and practice:

> My child, if you accept my words and treasure up my commandments within you, making your ear attentive to wisdom and inclining your heart to understanding; if you indeed cry out for insight and raise your voice for understanding; if you seek it like silver, and search for it as for hidden treasures – then you will understand the fear of the LORD and find the knowledge of God. (Proverbs 2.1–5)

What place prayer, waiting on God and listening to what he has to say plays in reflection in collaborative ministry will probably depend on the tradition and context of the ministry but a dialogue between experience, theory and theology can provide some of the most rounded insights.

Sharon was part of a peer support group and when the group met each member would be given the opportunity to share an ongoing issue within their work. It could be a problem, concern, dilemma or reflection, good or bad. On one occasion Sharon shared a conflict with her training minister that was causing her significant stress. The group listened carefully and began to ask sensitive questions trying to get below the surface of the issue. In response to one of these questions, Sharon suddenly blurted out, 'He just reminds me so much of the way my dad talked to me.' At this point another member of the group asked gently, 'Do you think that's why you might be reacting so strongly to what he says to you?' Sharon suddenly realized that her response to the minister carried with it much of the pain she had experienced in childhood, when she had received little encouragement and much criticism from her father. This realization encouraged her to seek help in working through her childhood experiences and made a huge difference in her relationship with the minister, as she was able to separate her childhood experiences from her current relationship.

Reflection and collaborative ministry

Reflective skills can help support collaborative ministry in a number of ways:

- It gives a framework to explore personal experiences within a larger setting.
- It provides tools to examine practice and processes as a team.
- Reflection accesses corporate wisdom.
- Reflecting before, during and after collaboration gives opportunities to maximize learning.
- Theological reflection gives a Christian framework to ask questions of ministry.
- It may save us from hasty, knee-jerk or other inappropriate reactions.
- It gives a process for processing problems, worries, personal and corporate dilemmas, etc. that might otherwise not be processed.
- It aids professional, ministerial and spiritual formation.

Points for reflection, discussion and action

- Is reflection an integral part of your practice? If not, why not?
- Where are you on John's layers of reflection continuum? What do you need to do to move on to the next level?

- What is a recent incident or issue that would benefit from reflection time? Why?
- What is your default resource for theological reflection? Can you start with your experience or do you tend to begin with the Bible or theology?
- What opportunities are there to introduce corporate reflection?

5

Vision-building skills

A shared vision is not an idea. It is not even an important idea such as freedom. It is rather, a force in people's hearts, a force of impressive power. It may be inspired by an idea, but once it goes further – if it is compelling enough to acquire the support of more than one person – then it is no longer an abstraction. It is palpable. People begin to see it as if it exists. Few, if any, forces in human affairs are as powerful as shared vision.

(Senge, 2006, p. 192)

Vision has been defined as 'the ability to think about or plan the future with imagination or wisdom' (*New Oxford American Dictionary*, 2005) or hopefully with imagination *and* wisdom! Malphurs believes that:

Vision is crucial to any ministry. Ministry without a vision is like a surgeon without a scalpel, a cowboy who has lost his horse, a carpenter with a broken hammer. To attempt ministry without a clear well articulated vision is to invite a stillbirth. (1999, p. 17)

Statements like this suggest that vision-building is essential.

In true collaborative ministry we build vision together rather than assuming that the leader has the vision that others should follow, the classic model in many leadership books, both Christian and secular. Jenny talks about how she was invited to join the outreach team at a local project because they thought having a youth worker on the team would be 'great'. However, the project manager didn't actually explain to her why they wanted a youth worker on the team and she was left unclear about her role in the wider vision of the project. Although the idea for collaborative ministry may start with just one person, hopefully, the shape, purpose and outworking will evolve as people come together to explore it.

This is how the Centre for Youth Ministry <www.centreforyouth ministry.ac.uk> began. Bob Mayo had a vision of integrating good professional youth work practice with people's passion for youth ministry but then, together with Pete Ward, drew together a diverse group of people who gave birth to the vision. It has become the largest UK provider of full-time youth and community work undergraduate education and at the time of writing has nine organizations as partners delivering professionally qualifying youth and community work courses at further education, undergraduate and postgraduate levels. A spark of inspiration can lead to so much!

It was important that others were brought in quickly as people are much more likely to become committed to a vision if they have had a chance to shape it. As Sofield and Juliano note: 'Where the people affected by the vision are not involved in formulating it, the predicted outcome is apathy' (1987, p. 73). Sometimes clergy can be surprised that people do not have the enthusiasm for a vision that they had hoped for but often that is because they have imposed a vision onto their congregation rather than built it with them. We quickly lose interest in a church or organization if we have nothing invested and vision is a good starting point for investment.

Vision is a word that is sometimes used interchangeably with mission. Mission is the overarching purpose of an organization, for example, Youth for Christ's <www.yfc.co.uk> is 'taking good news relevantly to every young person in Britain'. The vision says how this will be accomplished and changes over time as vision becomes reality and a new vision is required. If we are unclear about our mission it may be worthwhile spending some time refining it before starting the vision-building process or we may be happy to adopt a general statement such as 'to know God and make him known' or 'to worship God and show the love of Jesus in action as well as words' that will be relevant to a range of future scenarios.

We then need a vision to help us put our mission into practice. In the spirit of collaborative ministry the invitation to a vision-building process may be best if it is inclusive rather than being seen as the responsibility of an elite. In a particularly large church or organization it may be best to build vision in different areas before coming together with perhaps representatives of each group who bring a variety of perspectives.

Knowing who to involve in the vision-building process can be difficult. Any church or organization has many stakeholders who have an interest in what they do. Identifying who they are and what their part in the bigger picture is needs to be done before starting the process. The broader the range of stakeholders that take part, the more likely it is that the whole picture is seen. In an activity identifying who the stakeholders are for youth workers, we got to 20-plus. A broadly based group may have many more. We can ask what stakeholders expect of and contribute to the church or organization and then identify those that need to be involved in the process because they are essential to what is done.

As with everything in ministry, we bring who we are to the vision-building process and it may be beneficial for each person or group involved to say very succinctly what their hopes, fears, assumptions and expectations are. Making such things explicit can help avoid misunderstanding and tension as different agendas are understood rather than being hidden. Personality also impacts our approach to vision. Sally is a big-picture person who often enjoys looking to the future but is an introvert who tends to work things out in her head and hasn't always talked about an idea before coming out with it. Although Paul is a detail person he tends to enjoy life in the present. This means we need to listen really carefully to each other and to value where each other is coming from. Paul tells a story of how he and Sally were once chatting about a forthcoming move to Birmingham when Sally (foolishly) said, 'I'd like to move to Plymouth after we've been to Birmingham.' Paul felt as if all his anchor points had disappeared; he didn't know what was happening, they hadn't even moved to Birmingham yet. Sally wasn't saying let's not go to Birmingham but it was as if she had done Birmingham in her head and was looking at what's next. Paul was frustrated but Sally couldn't see the problem – what's wrong with dreaming about the future? That's why you need skilled facilitation and an understanding of process when you do vision-building, to help avoid unnecessary stress!

Theological perspectives for vision-building

While there is much that can be learnt from the latest thinking in management and leadership, for many, having a biblical or theological rationale for what they do is more important. Here we suggest some biblical principles as an underpinning for vision-building which we have taken from Jesus' farewell discourse (John 13—17). There are several reasons for choosing this passage as a basis for vision-building. One is its future orientation, as 'the vision of the future in

John 13—17 embraces both the immediate future and a future beyond that future' (Stibbe, 1993, p. 142). Another is the challenge it provides to 'human systems of management, control and hierarchy' (Burridge, 1998, p. 167). Wright shows what this means in reality and encapsulates the sort of attitude that is helpful for all in collaborative ministry. He argues that Jesus establishes a pattern (John 13.15) and the implications are that 'the truly Christlike leader is known by the ease and spontaneity with which he or she does the little, annoying, messy things . . . the things which in our world we always secretly hope someone else will do so we won't have to waste our time, to demean ourselves' (2002, p. 48). It is sometimes doing these things that make collaborative ministry and vision-building work.

The principles:

- Right attitudes are essential. Mutual respect, openness, humility, vulnerability and interdependence are all encouraged and modelled by Jesus and if we begin with the right attitude this goes a long way to overcoming some of the barriers that there always are when looking at change and new pathways.
- Servant leadership needs to prepare the people for a process in the same spirit that Jesus washed his disciples' feet before the meal.
- Vision-building in collaborative ministry is a shared experience and preconceived ideas about how God may want to speak or act should be jettisoned.
- The way that we treat each other in this (and other aspects of collaborative ministry) will be a significant witness to others. We can still disagree with each other but there are ways that this can be done that show respect and a willingness to listen and a heart to build towards consensus and give the process the time it needs.
- Believe that God wants to work in and through us and will give us vision as we ask and seek him. Vision can come through any or all of us, in collaborative ministry we are not expecting a leader to present a vision that we assent to (or not).
- The Holy Spirit is with us in the process and we can look for a sense of peace as a sign of her presence.
- Sometimes we need to take down before we rebuild – pruning is an essential part of a fruitful garden and is not failure as we sometimes perceive, it's preparation for the season to come.

- Remember to have appropriate hope too – Jesus says, 'Take courage; I have conquered the world' (John 16.33). We do not mean this as a triumphalist statement but as one that encourages us to believe when God reveals to us something outside of our current comfort zone, faith level or experience.
- We are sent into the world just as the disciples were; keep mission and building the kingdom as central to the vision.

Elaborating such principles at the beginning of the process can help build shared values and understanding of what may well be a new way of doing things.

As well as providing principles, the Bible is also a good source of vision statements. Cormack (1995, p. 96) suggests that St Paul offers vision statements in most of his letters, often framed in the form of a prayer because they are dependent on God. They include:

- Let us work for the good of all (Galatians 6.10).
- Lead lives worthy of the Lord (Colossians 1.10).
- Live in peace (2 Corinthians 13.11).
- That your love may overflow more and more (Philippians 1.9).

What does a vision look like?

A vision should be: clear, comprehensible, simple, shared, imaginable/conceivable, desirable, feasible, realistic, flexible, dynamic, liquid, meaningful, understandable, communicable, owned. Visions can encompass both what we do and who we are. With a church the latter may be a more appropriate approach. Vision statements work best when they are inclusive, can be owned by all and are outward-looking. Once a vision has been agreed there is a need for a way of achieving the vision to be identified that includes specific goals and objectives to achieve them. Objectives tend to be most effective when developed using the SMART formula – specific, measurable, achievable, realistic and timed. So, for example, a SMART objective might be to establish by next September a toddler group which provides space for parents and carers to offer each other support and supervised play opportunities for their children.

Brierley (1989, pp. 188–9) has some helpful advice about how to communicate the vision which is helpful to bear in mind while we are developing it:

- Write the vision initially in one sentence – this is the core concept.
- Use familiar and accessible words.
- Ensure words are clear and unambiguous.
- Use active and doing verbs rather than passive ones.
- Be as short and crisp as possible.
- State one idea at a time. Do not put two ideas into one sentence.
- Frame the sentence in the positive.
- State the particular and not the general.
- You are aiming for a response. Therefore be specific.
- Focus on the future, not the past.

Vision-building processes and tools

There are a variety of ways in which we can approach the vision-building process. Nigel Roberts of Youth for Christ shared with us a great opening activity: with everyone in a small group, ask each person to think of an animal they would like to create by tearing it a piece at a time from an A4 sheet of paper. They are not to tell anyone else what animal they are trying to create. Each group is given a sheet of paper and each person is allowed an inch tear before passing the sheet on to the next person. After a minute or so collect in all the torn animals and ask other groups to identify them. Invariably they can't. Run the exercise again, this time each group agrees to all make the same animal. The tearing starts one inch at a time but usually at the end the animals are recognized. This is a simple way of communicating that if we follow our individual vision the end result is a mess. Within a Christian context we tend to underpin the process with prayer and allow time for listening to God. The other thing to bear in mind is the need to reflect on the 'signs of the times' to ensure that we are taking the wider cultural context into account (Luke 21.29–30).

Some other suggestions for exercises follow; choose and adapt them for your own situation.

Picturing the future

Equipment Flip-chart-size paper, magazines, spray mount or glue, scissors, felt tips, masking tape.

Process

1 We begin by exploring where we are now before moving on to where we would like to be. Divide up into groups of four or five. This may be within areas or across areas depending on how we want to do the vision-building. There are arguments for people who already work together in a specific area to work to their focus; there is merit but also in cross-fertilization of ideas across different areas.

Give the group 15 minutes to work together to produce a collage from pictures in a magazine and using felt tips to represent where they think the church or organization is at currently. Give each group five minutes to explain their picture, collating a list of key words and concepts on a flip chart as you go along. Ensure these are recorded for later distribution. Appointing a recorder for the session may be useful.

2 In the same groups, repeat the process but ask the groups to produce a picture of how they see the agency at a specific time in the future, say one, two, five or ten years, depending on where we are now and what we are hoping to achieve in the process.

Again ask each group to explain their picture and then, if possible, put them up around the room using masking tape. Ask the whole group to identify common elements or themes and ideas that they want to explore further. These can form the basis of a vision. Ensure that each member of the group has a copy of lists from pictures 1 and 2 to reflect on and pray over if you are doing the next stage at a later date.

3 Ask the question, 'How do we get from here to there?' The first part of this may be to clarify where 'there' is. This may be done in the form of four to eight statements that represent where we want to get to. Once this is done each of the statements needs to be broken down and objectives set. Along with this it may be possible to identify principles which underpin the statements and give a glimpse as to how as a church or organization we need to work together to achieve the vision.

Telling our story and writing the next chapter

Equipment Flip-chart paper, marker pens or an electronic equivalent.

Process

1 Choose an appropriate length of time in the past – this will depend on how long the church or organization has been in existence and who is part of the vision-building group. Draw a line across the centre of a landscape page. Put the start date on the left-hand side and the current date on the right-hand side. Identify important events from the past and put them above, below or on the line depending on whether they were positive or negative events.

2 Identify a list of key words and phrases which describe where the church or organization is at now. This may be done as a group or we can ask people to write their ideas on individual post-it notes and stick them up. We then use this material to craft a paragraph which says who we are and what we do, and gives some of the reasons for this.

3 Choose a specific time in the future, e.g. one, two, five or ten years, and ask people to describe what they hope things will be like then. For example, What sort of church might we be in five years' time? How would we want to be known locally? Who would be part of us? What would we be doing? What would we be like? Tell the story as if from five years in the future when the church is looking back at how it has developed.

4 Take the main elements from this process and turn it into a series of vision statements. For example, 'We will be a church that is known in the community as people who care and who are there to listen and offer a helping hand' or 'We are an organization that helps local people make their voice heard to those who make policy.' Now plan how you are going to get there using the SMART objectives described above.

God's questions

Cormack (1999, pp. 235–45) has an approach to vision-building that is based on six sessions, usually done over two separate days, where each session looks to answer one question that God asked of his people in the Old Testament.

1 *Where are you? Genesis 3.8*
  Each participant chooses words or phrases to summarize the organization in the past, present and future – one for each stage. Each person's answer is then listed on a flip chart and as a group

themes are identified that reflect the organization in each phase. These emerging themes help to provide an overview of where the organization is at.

2 *What is in your hand? Exodus 4.2*
In answering this question participants need to list what assets there are in these eight areas:

- resources
- relationships
- activities
- culture
- systems
- people
- structures
- public image.

Within this the organization should be able to identify strengths and weaknesses and be aware of what they have to take into the future vision.

3 *What are you doing here? 1 Kings 19.9*
This question is getting at what the organization is actually doing, how time is being used and once this has been done trying to categorize the different answers to provide an overview of the organization's activities.

4 *What do you see? Zechariah 4.2*
The response to this question involves looking forward and seeing what might be. Asking this question from the perspective of a range of stakeholders will give you the big picture. Cormack (1999, p. 242) suggests that 80 per cent of your future success is dependent on only 20 per cent of your stakeholders. Having identified the stakeholders, ask what would they want more of and less of in five or ten years' time. Another approach is to ask people to answer an open-ended question such as 'In ten years' time we . . .' and then analyse the results, which are likely to be the core of the vision when synthesized into a succinct sentence or two.

5 *Can these bones live? Ezekiel 37.3*
This is the stage at which the vision needs to be tested and turned into a viable strategy that can work by identifying clear goals and objectives.

6 *Who will go for us? Isaiah 6.8*

This is the point at which you need to assess and solicit personal commitment to the vision. The vision needs to be disseminated beyond the team that has developed it (although best practice involves trying to include as many as possible in the vision-building process). It may be that this question is best answered really early on in the process and then these people work through the other questions before disseminating the vision.

Resources and responsibilities

Another way of approaching vision-building is to look at what we already have in terms of resources and responsibilities and look at how this may change in the future. The key questions that need to be asked would be:

1 What is the situation now in this area?
2 How do we think it will be at a specific point in the future?
3 Why do we think it will be like this?
4 If we don't like the predicted outcome, what can we do to change it?
5 How do we get to where we want to be?

Areas to include:

- staff (including volunteers)
- buildings and equipment
- finance
- people or service users
- community (context in which we serve)
- service provided
- structure of organization and leadership
- image/perception of the organization from a range of perspectives.

(This approach is based on an idea in Brierley, 1989, pp. 146–50.)

Future search conference

This is the name of a model developed by Weisbord (1992) and works on the principle that everybody (a term that encompasses a broad cross-section of stakeholders) works on the whole system and that we focus on trying to build common ground that everyone can commit to without feeling that they are compromising. In relation to vision-building, the process would consist of something like this:

1 *Review of the past*
   With a review of the past we need to identify an appropriate time span and agree what will be reviewed. The history of the church or organization needs to be done but it may also be useful to look at both changes in society and the people there. The idea of 'milestones' may help us to focus on what is important rather than getting bogged down in unnecessary detail. Drawing a timeline is often the easiest way of collating this information.

2 *External forces shaping our lives and institutions now*
   The idea of this phase is to get a shared understanding of the current context. It can be done by brainstorming ideas, writing them on a flip chart, displaying the results around the room and then identifying the trends that are emerging that might be influential and relevant to our particular organization.

3 *Internal factors: things we are proud of and things we are sorry for*
   What do we want to take forward? What do we want to leave behind? This can be approached by asking people to discuss these areas in twos and threes and then using post-it notes to put the outcome of their discussions on the appropriate flip-chart sheet. The results of this phase should be displayed too.

4 *Future ideal scenario*
   This phase needs to focus on creativity and innovation and draws on the outcome of the previous three phases. Where possible have the progress so far displayed around the room to feed into this phase. Working in small groups, encourage participants to imagine what they would like the future to look like at a specified point in the future. After a set period of time pass the ideas round the different groups for feedback and then work all together and try and collate the best elements and gain consensus around a future scenario that everyone can commit to.

5 *Action-planning*
   Once the future scenario has been agreed the next stage is to design specific strategies to achieve this. Again, try brainstorming in small groups to identify relevant strategies and pass the strategies around the different groups for comment. Finally in the large

group agree which strategies seem to be the best and form them into SMART objectives. The final task will be to agree a review and implementation process.

To achieve all of this may take a couple of days and is best led by experienced facilitators who understand group processes. For something like this two facilitators are good as they can compare notes, agree on interventions or programme changes and each take responsibility for either the process or the content. How something like this happens is often as important as what happens. There are merits in using external facilitators who can help you with the process as this helps with the presumption of everyone being equal and can make it easier for people to voice their ideas than if the main leader(s) are facilitating.

Metaphors

Developing metaphors can be an insightful way of getting us to identify the sort of people, church or organization we are but also what we want to be. Metaphors can sometimes help get under the surface of people's perceptions and give us the possibility of exploring vision in a way that resonates with people for whom more usual processes don't work as well. These are some metaphors for churches (from Hare, cited in Lovell, 2000, pp. 303–4) or organizations which, if committed to, engender very different ways of being:

> Family of God; Vineyard; Community of faith; Body of Christ; Community resource; Community conscience; Pilgrim people; Base for mission; Holy place; Worship theatre; Circus ring; Place of healing; Place of refuge; Preparation for heaven.

Organizational ones can be developed around a series of initial ideas or contexts:

> Hospital or Field Hospital, Emergency Room, Surgery; Nursery, Playground, Theme Park, Fairground; Harbour, Lighthouse, Lifeboat.

Sport, Nature, Media, and the Military all provide rich ground for metaphors too.

To use metaphors in vision-building get the process flowing by putting a few ideas on strips of paper and then asking people to add their own. Next, individuals or small groups choose the three metaphors that are most like the church or organization and one that is the least like it. Collate and display the result to everyone and then use the metaphors to try to develop one specifically for your church or organization. You can also use some common metaphors such as a house (foundations, windows, doors, roof, walls, rooms, attic, basement, etc.) or tree (roots, trunk, branches, leaves) where you label different parts and explore vision through that medium.

What business?

One of the simplest ways of exploring vision is taking further something we first heard at a John Wimber conference. There are four simple questions:

1 What business are you in?
2 How's business?
3 What business do you want to be in?
4 What do you need to do then?

Conclusion

Essentially in vision-building you identify a vision, develop the strategy and communicate the vision. The chapters on groups, facilitation and conflict will help you deal with some of the issues that will inevitably emerge during the process. However, the process on its own is not enough; the vision needs to be maintained. There needs to be an ongoing commitment to the vision to see it through rather than it just being a piece of paper that gets filed away and dusted down for a funding bid or promotional brochure. Maintaining the vision means keeping it at the forefront of people's minds, referring to it, having it displayed publicly and making sure that what you take on fits with where God is leading you.

Points for reflection, discussion and action

- Can we articulate our mission and vision clearly?
- Is it known and owned more widely within the church or organization and stakeholders?
- Are we at the stage of needing a new vision?
- Which metaphor resonates? Is there a different metaphor that seems better?

- How have we built vision in the past? What are the strengths and weaknesses of this approach?
- Which of the approaches to vision-building listed seems right for us?
- In what ways can we be more collaborative in our vision-building?

6

Teamwork skills

Teams are very difficult to create. They are tougher to motivate. They are impossible to predict. They can be challenging to lead. They can inspire greatness and they can embody pettiness. They can gel quickly and they can splinter apart overnight. They are filled with people who are unique in their backgrounds, hurts, needs, joys, desires, gifts, aspirations, and call. To get a diverse group of people working on the same page is the ongoing priority and challenge for leaders. (Macchia, 2005, p. 17)

Virtually any ministry which is collaborative on an ongoing basis will involve some kind of teamwork. Perhaps there will be several teams each with a specific role, and many people involved in collaborative ministry may find themselves leading or being part of a number of teams simultaneously. Anyone who has been part of a team for any length of time will have experienced some of the highs and lows highlighted by Macchia above. Teamwork can be one of the most rewarding, but also one of the most frustrating experiences in ministry.

Various writers have sought to define teams and to highlight the difference between teams and groups. Babbington Smith describes a team as:

A group in which the individuals have a common aim and in which the jobs and skills of each member fit with those of others, as – to take a very mechanical and static analogy – in a jigsaw puzzle pieces fit together without distortion and together produce some overall pattern. (in Adair, 1986, p. 95)

Katzenbach and Smith echo aspects of this, defining a team as: 'a small number of people with complementary skills who are committed to a common purpose, performance goals, and approach for which they hold themselves mutually accountable' (1996, p. 45).

Two common factors in this definition, and in others, are the sense of a common task or purpose and the complementary nature of group members' contributions. Macchia's understanding of team in a Christian ministry context also picks up on this:

> A Christian ministry team is a manageable group of diversely gifted people who hold one another accountable to serve joyfully together for the glory of God by:
>
> • sharing a common mission
> • embodying the loving message of Christ
> • accomplishing a meaningful ministry
> • anticipating transformative results.   (Macchia, 2005, p. 41)

Adair sees teams as 'work groups' (1986, p. 14), whereas Katzenbach and Smith are keen to highlight the difference between teams and working groups, suggesting that working groups 'rely on the sum of "individual bests" for their performance' and 'pursue no collective work products requiring joint effort' (1996, p. 85). Their 'team performance curve' shows clearly the differences they perceive and is helpful in our consideration of when a group becomes a team. They see the following potential stages or possibilities (1996, pp. 91–2):

• working group – which meets to share information, good practice or perspectives but has little common purpose, collaborative working or mutual accountability;
• pseudo-team – which has the potential to perform as a team but lack of common purpose and goals means it never achieves this;
• potential team – which is seeking to improve performance but requires more clarity around purpose and goals and more discipline in collaborative working;
• real team – which is a mutually accountable group with complementary skills, equally committed to common purpose, goals and approaches;
• high-performance team – as above but members are highly committed to one another's growth and success.

In a ministry context, we should be operating in one of these last two areas to demonstrate true collaborative working. Bex provides a good example of these latter stages and tells how she was part of a team taking a large group to Soul Survivor. Two days after they arrived it rained solidly for 24 hours and camping at the bottom of the hill did not bode well for the group. One of the tents sleeping 12 flooded. The wails of young girls finding their hair straighteners in a pool of muddy water echoed round the site. The team of leaders got to work. Together they cleared out the tent, putting stuff in tents that were not flooded, sandbagged tents that were vulnerable and erected a new tent at the top of the hill. Bex ended up sitting in a tent with two girls trying to calm them down and reassuring them the mud would wash out and that in a few years' time they would look back at this and laugh! If we find ourselves in a working group, pseudo-team or potential team, it is important to consider how we might use the skills outlined in the rest of this chapter to develop and grow the team so that it can begin to perform to its full potential.

In an individualistic culture, teamwork is fundamental and most people would acknowledge that teams are generally likely to accomplish more than individuals. However, although people recognize the importance of teamwork, pressures around time, money and familiar ways of working (for example, a focus on individual productivity, lack of training and development) often mean teamwork is neglected. Similarly, many organizations and churches have created a culture in which competitiveness rather than collaboration is the norm.

Sometimes the impression is given that teams just happen, but they don't. Just as any relationship requires an investment of time and energy, so teams need strategic thinking, personal investment, nurture and time if they are to be effectively developed, and maintained.

Theological perspectives

There are numerous examples of teamwork in the Bible, which give snapshots of how teams can work effectively and where they can go wrong. When Moses highlights his weakness in public-speaking to God, Aaron is called alongside him to work collaboratively with him and speak on his behalf (Exodus 4.14). This is highly effective in much of their ministry, but some of the pain of teamworking is illustrated too when Aaron and Miriam turn against Moses and grumble about him behind his back (Numbers 12.1–15).

In the book of Nehemiah we see a further example of teamwork as the walls of Jerusalem are rebuilt. Nehemiah's vision to rebuild the city (Nehemiah 1.5) is one that he could not possibly accomplish alone. Instead we see individuals and families working together to accomplish the task collaboratively, taking responsibility for specific parts of the task (3.28–32), standing together against opposition (4.13), addressing conflicts and injustices that arise (5.1–12) and gathering together to worship, pray and celebrate their achievements (8.1–12).

In Jesus' life and ministry we also see teamwork encouraged. The group of disciples that he draws around him lives, travels and works together. Although this team is by no means perfect, with the occasional argument over who is the greatest (Luke 9.43), we see some helpful illustrations of the advantages of teamwork. The disciples go out to minister in pairs (Luke 10), undertake practical tasks such as distributing food (Matthew 14.19) and spend time with Jesus learning and questioning together (Matthew 16.24; 13.10). At times individuals are sent off to do specific tasks (Matthew 21.1–2), sometimes only Peter, James and John go with Jesus (Matthew 17.1). On other occasions the group appears to work as a cohesive whole (Luke 8.22).

Identity and structure

The group processes explored in Chapter 2 do, of course, equally apply to team contexts. Awareness of development stages, culture, norms, roles and dynamics is crucial for those wishing to work effectively with teams. Part of the process of establishing and building a team is creating a sense of identity. Much of this will come from the team's sense of purpose – the vision and aims – but shared history, strong relational ties and the personal commitment of team members are also significant. Relational bonds can be strengthened through shared interests, shared vision, complementary personality types, effective communication or working together on a task. However we engender it, a sense of cohesiveness is crucial to effective teamwork. Even something relatively simple like the team's name can assist in giving identity and belonging.

Macchia (2005, p. 20) identifies five traits of a healthy team – trust, empowerment, assimilation, management and service – suggesting these need to be nurtured if teams are to function well. Shared values are important, even where there are differences in personality, preferred approaches and theological perspectives.

During her professional training, Jenny, a church-based youth work student, became increasingly committed to values of empowerment and participation. As she became aware of the very hierarchical leadership structure in her church, she found herself increasingly conflicting with others during team meetings. As her values changed, this affected her relationships with others in the team and when she graduated she found a job with a Christian organization, which more fully reflected her values.

In our experience it is possible to have different values within a team, but it can make life more difficult and can mean more conflict, which has the potential to be creative but needs to be handled sensitively and appropriately.

Team structure will depend on its context and aims. Numbers may vary, but the word 'manageable' in Macchia's definition earlier is important in this regard. If a team is too small it may be unable to achieve its objectives because there are insufficient people to do the work. If a team is too large, communication becomes more complex, participation is more challenging and collaborative decision-making more problematic. Dynamics like subgrouping, scapegoating and splitting are more likely to emerge and power struggles can be more common (see Chapter 2 on groupwork).

Aims

Having a clear sense of direction is vital. We have already explored the importance of a collaborative approach to identifying and communicating vision. In ministry contexts aims and objectives are often tacit – leaders may have a sense of what they want to see, but this may not be formulated in ways that can be understood and communicated. For effective collaborative working, everyone within the team must have a clear understanding of what they are seeking to achieve. We should not assume that this is obvious – it must be articulated, and articulated in ways that are both understandable and memorable. This might include discussing and reviewing aims regularly, pinning them up on a wall and using them as a focus for prayer and evaluation.

Aims should be set in the context of the core purpose and vision to enable team members to see the 'big picture'. They should be achievable but not too easily achievable, having an element of challenge within them. This will serve as a motivating factor to those involved. Clear, challenging aims tend to generate enthusiasm and energy. Katzenbach and Smith (1996, p. 12) relate their understanding of team closely to performance. Although there are many other benefits of being part of teams – belonging and satisfaction – they see this desire to perform and achieve results as the most important issue. Using some of the vision-building ideas from the previous chapter will help this.

Team leadership

In our consideration of approaches to leadership in Chapter 1, we identified a spectrum of styles from laissez-faire through to autocratic (see Table 1.1 on p. 13). In team-building, different styles will be required at different times. Organizational culture is likely to influence how people lead and we will develop our own preferred styles and methods. Part of the art of effective team leadership is knowing when and how to adopt different but appropriate approaches. We have already emphasized our preference for a facilitative approach in collaborative work, but it is important to recognize that at times we will need to be more directive. Challenging discrimination, bullying, gossip or other unacceptable behaviour will call for an authoritarian response, as will concerns relating to health and safety and safeguarding (child protection). Leaders may also need to be directive in establishing and maintaining boundaries within the team, particularly in the forming stage and conflict situations, when individuals often need direction and support.

Leaders are likely to be the people who establish and have power to challenge and change the team's norms and culture. Who we are in this regard is as important as what we do. If we are competitive and ambitious we will probably create an individualistic, competitive team culture. Conversely, if we encourage, empower and celebrate the achievements of others, a co-operative culture should be engendered. In collaborative ministry, we strongly believe in leading by example. Those who do not model what they ask of others quickly lose the respect of their teams. In this respect self-awareness and integrity are key personal qualities for those in leadership. Similarly, an ability to trust and a sense of being trustworthy is important in establishing a sense of security. Having vision and an ability to inspire, motivate and encourage others is essential if the team is to progress and achieve.

Roles

Because teams are more task-oriented than many groups, clarity about roles and responsibilities is vital and we need to beware of 'role overload' (Adair, 1986, p. 37), where an individual is seeking to perform too many different roles and becomes overwhelmed. Belbin (1993, p. 17) draws on examples from the sporting world to highlight the importance of complementary roles: 'A good team comprises players who restrict their activities so as to avoid diminishing the role of others but who play their own role with distinction.' Seeing where people fit and ensuring they are working where they flourish is a key responsibility for team leaders.

Many of us have lots of things that we can do, some of which bring us alive but others which we may find emotionally draining. Jo talks about this in terms of working in a 'multicoloured' place or a 'black, white and grey' place. At certain times we will need to do the black, white and grey tasks, but we will be more fulfilled if the majority of our time is spent in our multicoloured places. The exciting thing about this is that multicoloured things will be different for each of us. For example, Sally would find it difficult to work with bereaved families, whereas Paul finds fulfilment in this. Conversely Sally enjoys writing detailed descriptors for new academic courses, whereas Paul would find this life-sapping. Good teamwork is about seeking to encourage people to flourish in their multicoloured places. This may mean being imaginative about the way we build our teams and who we invite to be involved. Many youth workers we know have really committed youth team members, who are not particularly skilled in relational youth work but enjoy helping with tuck shops, leading sports activities, playing chess or doing arts and crafts. Thinking creatively about the make-up of our team will sometimes give opportunity to people we may have not considered, or who might rule themselves out for all kinds of reasons.

Maureen was employed as an administrator for a community project. She had the qualifications and experience to do the job skilfully, but from her first day at work she struggled to fit in. She arrived late, took a long time over small tasks, made a lot of silly mistakes and didn't seem to have picked up the ethos of the project. After three years the funding for her post ran out but because she needed the money the project kept her on doing sessional work with parents and toddlers. Maureen appeared to transform virtually overnight. She was enthusiastic and outgoing. Her sessions were imaginative, creative, well-planned and thought through. The service users loved her and responded well to her. Given the right role in the team she became almost a different person. It's such a shame someone didn't spot right from the outset that Maureen was in the wrong job, but people were so frustrated with her lack of 'performance' in her initial role that they never considered that she might simply be unsuited to it.

Wisdom is needed here. Often it is simply not possible to have everyone doing jobs they love and values of serving and sacrifice remain important aspects of teamwork. However, good team leaders will assist team members to become more aware of their skills, interests and passions and will seek to take these into account as the team develops and grows.

Belbin's team roles

Belbin uses the term 'team role' to describe 'a tendency to behave, contribute and interrelate with others at work in certain distinctive ways' (1993, p. 24). In this definition an individual's team role might differ from the functional or 'official' role they have in a team. Ideally the two should overlap significantly, and becoming aware of our own preferred team roles and those of our team members should help in developing a better 'fit' of roles within the team. This model emphasizes and values diversity. Each team role is different and has areas of strength and allowable weakness (Belbin, 1993, p. 22).

Plants are creative, imaginative and unorthodox. They are 'ideas' people and are usually skilled at thinking 'outside the box', solving difficult problems and coming up with creative plans and suggestions. Plants may ignore details and get bored easily. They may also be too preoccupied with their own thoughts and ideas to communicate effectively with the rest of the team.

Resource investigators tend to be extrovert and enthusiastic. They are generally good communicators and are skilled in exploring opportunities and developing contacts outside the team. They can be over-optimistic when it comes to time management or goal-setting and will sometimes lose interest in something once their initial enthusiasm for it has passed.

Co-ordinators are mature and confident and will often be found in leadership roles. They are good at clarifying roles and making decisions and, because they can often see where people fit, they are good delegators. They can sometimes be perceived as manipulative and may delegate personal work that they should really do themselves.

Shapers are challenging and dynamic. They thrive on pressure and are quite task-focused. They have the courage and determination to overcome obstacles which may face the team but at times their drive and determination can hurt others and provoke negative reactions within the team.

Monitor evaluators are sober, strategic and discerning. They are able to see a situation from a range of viewpoints and are accurate in their judgements. They often lack the drive and ability to inspire or motivate others and can also come across as rather critical, but they are the team member most likely to stop the team making serious mistakes.

Team workers are co-operative, mild, perceptive and diplomatic. They tend to be people-focused and peacemaking in their approach and have good listening, communication and team skills. They can be easily influenced and are often eager to please, which may mean that they are indecisive at key times.

Implementers are disciplined, reliable and hardworking. They are the members of the team most likely to simply get on and get the job done. They are good at turning ideas into practical action but can be rather inflexible and may be reluctant to embrace new possibilities and opportunities.

Completers are conscientious and painstaking when it comes to undertaking work. They are good at searching out things that have been missed and spotting mistakes. They keep to task and are likely to complete work on time. They can be anxious, tend to worry and nitpick and are often reluctant to delegate work to others.

Specialists tend to contribute on only a narrow front and are single-minded and self-motivated. They provide experience, knowledge or skills in specific areas but are generally not interested in the big picture of what is going on. Often teams will draw in specialists at key times for a specific purpose.

Identifying team roles is not always easy. Several factors might affect how people function within the team – the perceived expectations of others, the task they have been assigned, their own sense of experience and security. People will often also behave differently if a leader or boss is present. Jo is a combination of plant, co-ordinator and shaper, but in certain teams has sometimes come across as a monitor evaluator and completer – two of her lowest-scoring roles! In these situations she adopted these roles because no one else in the team was doing them. However, getting stuck in these roles has sometimes led to significant frustration on her part and has prevented her from flourishing in her own areas of skill and passion.

Being explicit about team roles within a team can benefit team-building and the development of individual confidence and security. It is helpful to use a questionnaire (Belbin, 1981, pp. 147–52), discussing and exploring results together. This provides an opportunity for openness and relationship development within the team. It is critical to emphasize that the roles are equally important, as people tend to appreciate certain roles more than others. In church situations, people-focused roles (co-ordinator, resource investigator, team worker) are often valued more than task-oriented ones (monitor evaluator, completer). Another benefit of identifying team roles is growing our awareness of which roles are missing from the team. For example, teams which have no completer will need to take extra care to check that work is followed through if they are not to leave a swathe of unfinished projects in their wake. Having identified team roles we can encourage people to flourish in their strengths and make plans to cover potential gaps or weaknesses. We must, however, be cautious about stereotyping and putting people into boxes or labelling every behaviour as part of the team role. There is often a fine line between playing to a person's strengths and encouraging personal development.

Building or growing teams

Selecting or choosing team members can be an interesting process. Many leaders are tempted to choose team members 'in their own image' but if a team is to work effectively we need to be secure enough to select people whose skills and personalities are complementary rather than identical to our own. Areas of competence, availability, ability to work with others, values and potential will all be important and in ministry contexts character, integrity and spiritual maturity should also be taken into account. Sometimes it may be better to have team members who have less skill but more time, commitment and enthusiasm than highly skilled people who are unreliable or unmotivated.

We will rarely find ourselves in situations where we can immediately choose willing and available people with the exact skill-set, values and maturity that we are looking for, so a key aspect of choosing team members will be enabling individuals to develop into a role. The concept of 'growing' teams is as important as 'building' teams in ministry. A building metaphor suggests taking material that is already present and constructing and organizing it into a structure that is fit for purpose. A growing metaphor suggests more of an organic process. In a garden, plants are nurtured, fed, watered, supported by stakes, moved into different places and pruned to assist their growth. The garden which emerges is assisted by the work of the gardener but the process contains a high degree of unpredictability. Sudden frosts or blight can hinder growth or kill off new plants, while some seedlings might flourish unexpectedly and bear unforeseen flowers or fruit. Weeds might spring up and hinder new growth.

So it is with growing teams. Numerous internal and external factors can affect the way teams are started, developed and function. When selecting team members, identifying potential is a good starting point, but we will need to put in place support and opportunities for training and development. It is crucial to start with the team we have, not the team we wish we had. Recognizing and valuing the strengths and weaknesses of our team members will help us avoid an 'if only' attitude, which can so easily turn into resentment and frustration.

Task, individual, team

Developing teams will necessitate considering the three areas outlined in Adair's three-circle model (see Figure 1.1 on p. 14) – the task or skills needed to accomplish the task, the needs and development of individuals and the development of the team as a corporate unit.

Clarifying aims, allocating and delegating roles and responsibilities, actual work planning, implementation and evaluation will all form part of the task-focused areas of team life. Tasks allocated to team members should be meaningful and valued – appreciating the unseen contributions of team members who are undertaking the less glamorous aspects of the team's responsibilities can significantly help morale. People generally want to feel needed. Delegation is important but needs to be done effectively. It is not enough to simply 'dump' tasks on people – clear instructions around expectations need to be given and where necessary, training, support and encouragement made available.

Skills development overlaps into the area of individual need and may require specific input. Bringing in specialists at certain times and exploring different approaches to training will be helpful here. These might include mentoring or coaching, on-the-job training, accessing external courses, offering support and supervision and building confidence through encouragement. Euan and Jane use the first week of each term for a training or team-building session for their youth work team; they meet at the same time and on the same night as the youth group usually meets so that the team members are available. If people are to grow they need opportunities to try new things and develop their skills in environments which feel supportive and affirming. Learning will also be more effective if we create a team culture where honest feedback is given and received.

When it comes to the third area – that of growing the sense of cohesion within the team – we need to consider when and how often we will meet together. This includes thinking through the level of commitment required, people's availability and identifying meeting times which work for everyone concerned. Contracting and boundary-setting give opportunity to explore expectations. Providing opportunities for team members to grow their relationships and spend time together socially will usually make for better working relationships. Spending time in corporate prayer, team-building activities, away days, engaging in study, exploring core beliefs or even watching a film together can all assist in engendering a sense of cohesion and mutuality. We cannot underestimate the importance of attitude in growing teams – simple things like not taking people for granted, treating people with respect and expressing appreciation and thanks may seem obvious but are often forgotten in the busyness of church and organizational life.

Thinking about all these different things may seem at times a little daunting, but developing effective teams requires a significant investment of time and energy. If we are taking over the leadership of a team we may need to address issues around established culture and norms. Time may be needed to explore or revisit core issues around purpose, values and expectations. Sometimes it may be advantageous to end one team and begin again from scratch, although this will need to be done sensitively and collaboratively, recognizing that some individuals may have a significant emotional investment in the original team.

Communication

Within any team it is essential to find ways of communication that are effective and that connect with every team member. Many teams now use email to share information, but care should be taken that everyone is on email – or checks it regularly – otherwise certain individuals will end up feeling that they hear everything later than everyone else or not at all. Face-to-face meetings will normally be important for most teams and we need to ensure that the time in these is used as effectively as possible. People need to feel that the investment of their time and energy is worthwhile. This can particularly be an issue when some people in the team are paid by the church or organization and others are doing demanding full-time jobs on top of their voluntary ministry. Having spent a whole day in their workplace it can often be incredibly frustrating to come to a team meeting which ends up being unfocused and unproductive.

Team leaders will normally take a key role in communication, although if this is an area of weakness it may be appropriate to delegate it. Where the team leader is the key communicator it is vital to ensure that communication is fair and 'democratic'. If one person in the team always receives information second-hand they can feel excluded or unvalued. Similarly, situations can arise where it feels as if the team leader has an 'in-crowd' with whom they discuss important issues prior to the team meeting. In terms of the use of technology, we would generally recommend that emails, text messages and letters generally be used for information purposes, rather than to seek to resolve or raise contentious issues. This will be explored further in Chapter 8.

Some potential hazards

Teams will inevitably hit difficulties. In some contexts people may belong to a team simply because of their job or role but may not actually want to be in it and their values and attitudes may differ considerably from those of others in the team. Power struggles, personality clashes, misunderstandings and poor communication may contribute to conflict within the team, which will then need to be addressed, but may be painful for all involved. Inherited teams can be particularly difficult, where we start in a new post and have to live with the history of all that has gone before and the way the team has been previously led. Some of the ideas in this and other chapters may help reform or renew the team if it is problematic.

Issues of favouritism or nepotism are important to mention specifically in this context as they can cause hurt, resentment and mis-understanding. Many of us will have come across situations where someone appears to have been given a role because they are related to or friends with the team leader. We heard of one situation where a church worship leader was encouraged to step aside from his responsibilities to focus on other areas of ministry. He did this reluctantly because he loved to lead worship, but wanted to be account-able to the minister. He was incredibly hurt later to discover that the minister's brother had then been given the responsibility of leading worship. However well intentioned we may be, those of us involved in leading teams need to be self-aware enough to realize when our relational connections with someone might blind us to our own bias. Collaborative approaches are very helpful here as participative decision-making around these kinds of issues is likely not only to prevent us making serious errors of judgement but will also give us a level of accountability which should help avoid even the accus-ation of favouritism or nepotism. Awareness of good practice around equal opportunities in personnel issues can be helpful here and vital for projects where external funding is being sought.

Teamwork is potentially one of the most rewarding aspects of col-laborative ministry and offers huge potential for all involved. Done well, it is likely to assist our own growth and development as well as being socially and emotionally rewarding. Done badly, much hurt and pain can be caused. The investment made in building and growing teams may appear costly but is certainly worthwhile.

Points for reflection, discussion and action

- Which of Kazenbach and Smith's stages of a team do you think you are at? How could you progress?

- In your experience of teamwork, how effective do you think the leadership provided has been? What has helped or hindered this?
- Looking at what you do at the moment, which activities make you feel in a 'multicoloured' place and which feel 'black, white and grey'?
- Reflecting on the list of team roles, what would you identify as your main roles? How are these currently being outworked in the teams you belong to?
- What things would help the teams you currently are part of in terms of the three areas of the task, individuals and team maintenance?

7

Supervision skills

There was a famous monastery that had fallen on hard times. Formerly its buildings were filled with young monks and the sound of chants and singing, but now it was deserted. People no longer came there to be nourished by prayer, worship or community. Only a handful of old monks shuffled through the cloisters and they praised God with heavy hearts. Near the monastery was a wood and in the wood a rabbi had built a hut. One day the abbot of the monastery decided to visit the rabbi and open his heart to him. So, soon after morning prayer, the abbot set out towards the woods and the rabbi's hut. As the hut came into view the abbot saw the rabbi standing in the doorway with arms outstretched in welcome. The two men embraced each other like long-lost brothers. The rabbi invited the abbot into his hut. The rabbi said, 'You and your brothers are serving God with heavy hearts and you have come to me for wisdom and advice. I will give you the advice you require on one condition. When I tell you what it is I have to say you must promise me to repeat it only once. After that no one must say it aloud again.' The abbot agreed and the rabbi looked at him and said, 'The Messiah is among you'. The abbot left pondering the words he had heard.

The next morning, the abbot called his monks together in the main room. He told them he had been to visit the rabbi in the woods to receive wisdom from him on their situation. He explained to the other monks the condition the rabbi had put on the teaching. The abbot paused with the eyes of the other monks on him wondering what he might say. Eventually the abbot told them that the rabbi had said that the Messiah was among them. The monks were startled by this teaching. 'What could it mean?' they asked each other. 'Who could it be?' they asked. Could it be Brother John or Father Matthew or Brother Thomas? Could it be that I am the Messiah? They were all deeply puzzled by the rabbi's teaching. But no one ever mentioned it again.

As time went by, the monks began to treat one another with a very special reverence. There was a gentle, wholehearted and generous spirit among them now which was very hard to describe but very easy to notice. They lived with one another as people who had finally found something.

But they prayed and lived and read the Scriptures together as though they were looking for something. Occasionally visitors found themselves deeply moved by the life of these monks. Before long, people were coming from far and wide to be nourished by the prayer life and community of the monks, and men were asking to become a part of their life together in the community.   (Original author unknown)

If all supervision had such amazing consequences we would be very committed to the process! This is an example of what happens during supervision for some in ministry: we find someone whom we respect and think can help us, start meeting and things change, or if they don't change we at least cope better! The story is an example of what could be called non-managerial supervision, which is support from outside the church or organization, often the only realistic option for those who are the main church leader as there is not an obvious line manager to offer supervision. Different traditions or people use a variety of words for supervision or something they use as a substitute and we may have a spiritual director, soul friend, mentor, life coach or friend/peer that we meet with regularly to reflect. Within a church setting with more than one staff member, often the main minister will supervise other staff and heads of areas will supervise volunteers. Within an organization there will often be a structure where the designated line manager offers supervision to those who work for them. In youth work we recommend a non-managerial supervisor as well as the line manager.

Within collaborative ministry it can be beneficial to have a strategy for supervision to ensure that everyone has appropriate support. This can be individual or may be with the whole group. Supervision shouldn't be an optional extra. Good supervision can be transformative, it can make a difference to how we do our jobs or roles, how we feel about them and our ability to sustain ourselves in them.

Paul's experience in a parish was weekly line management meetings and then a monthly supervision session. Chantel sees her volunteer youth work team for one hour a term as a group for supervision and then sees each person for 20 minutes or so once a year to review their role. Raj organizes an away day once a year for those heading up each area of ministry in the church along with the elders and includes a session of group supervision that a denominational worker leads. He then sees each person for an hour or so once a term for one-to-one supervision. It is impossible to be prescriptive about length and frequency of meeting as much depends on the experience, role and context of both the supervisor and supervisee.

What is supervision?

A literal translation of the word supervision means overseeing but that gives a narrow explanation of what is involved and such a perception can be off-putting. Supervision should be so much more. Definitions of supervision vary depending on the context the author is writing about. These give a taste of the range:

> Pastoral supervision is a method of doing and reflecting on ministry in which a supervisor and one or more supervisees covenant together to reflect critically on their ministry as a way of growing into self-awareness, ministerial competence, theological understanding and Christian commitment. (Pohly, 1993, p. 75)

> Supervision is located within the context of a clearly defined relationship within the organization; is neither an event or a method, but an ongoing process. Supervision . . . recognises the inter-dependence of accountability, competence, professional development and personal support. (Morrison, 1996, p. 13)

There are four main tasks or functions of supervision:

- managerial/administrative, which includes accountability, evaluation, feedback;
- education, which includes professional development and providing or signposting resources;
- support, which includes providing emotional care and referring on if further help is needed;
- mediation, which may include advocacy, intervention and facilitating relationships.

In a ministry context we may want to add theological reflection to enable experiences and their meaning to be explored more holistically.

Sometimes we can define something by what it is not or should not be:

Family worker: I've been having difficulty with the way that some people are glaring at the toddlers in the

	service. Some of the parents are getting quite agitated and one has said she can't face coming back.
Minister:	Ah . . . Now tell me, how are you getting on with the IVF?
Family worker thinks:	That's what he starts asking when I am raising something difficult he doesn't want to deal with. That's not what supervision should be. He's blurring wanting to be my pastor and my manager and using the pastoral to try and distract and undermine me.
Youth worker:	I'm sorry I didn't get the supervision list to you. I've had a really tough week because there are lots of visitors at our house, I'm not feeling very well and I'm really missing my boyfriend.
Vicar:	I've made a list. We can use that one. Now the first item is next month's youth service.
Youth worker thinks:	What about looking after me? Can't you hear my cry for help? I need support.

The effect of poor supervision can stay with someone for a long time. Sally still remembers a supervision session she had as an 18-year-old which left her feeling she wasn't worth investing in as she was young and female and probably didn't have a long-term future with the organization she was working with.

One of the reasons we encounter difficulties with supervision is that it is a term that comes with baggage. Imagine your line manager is someone like David Brent from the television programme *The Office*, a boss it is hard to respect or look to for support and supervision. If we are introducing a supervision policy or strategy for the first time it can be worthwhile spending time exploring people's previous experiences and encouraging them to articulate their expectations, hopes and fears as well as being explicit about what will or will not be involved. It is an accepted policy in counselling and other professions that if you are offering supervision you should be receiving supervision yourself and it can be reassuring for those we are supervising to know this.

Attentive and active listening

Developing good listening skills is essential in supervision. Effective listening will be both attentive and active. Attentive listening is about being fully present for the person you are listening to. This means putting aside our own preoccupations, tasks, priorities and concerns and giving our full attention to the other person. Active listening is about engaging with the person actively. Feeding back with facial expressions or simple comments ('I see') or using reflective questions will show the other person that we really are listening and therefore encourage them to share more of their thoughts and feelings. It is important too not to spend valuable 'listening' time formulating our own mental responses to what is being said and to resist the temptation to interrupt with comments, defensive responses, advice or responding to their experience with a similar or worse one of our own. Our current experience suggests that turning phones off or to silent is vital otherwise we may spend the session speculating on who is sending all those text messages rather than focusing on the task at hand.

Responsibilities in supervision

Ideally a church or organization should provide time, space, resources and policies for supervision. Beyond this Hawkins and Shohet (2000, p. 118) identify the responsibilities of the individual supervisor and supervisee. As a supervisor we should ensure a safe place and have an approach that is supportive, encouraging and open. Bearing in mind the appropriate balance between management, education and support, we need to help supervisees explore and clarify thinking, feelings, plans, etc. and where necessary share our experience, information and skill. We need to be ready to challenge any practice that supervisees share which appears to be unethical, unwise or incompetent behaviour (although if we have observed this we should address it at the next available opportunity; supervision is not about discipline). Supervisors should also help develop self-awareness and challenge personal or professional blind spots.

As supervisees we have a responsibility to identify our own needs and make it clear what we want and expect from supervision. Although difficult for some of us, it can be helpful to start with an attitude of trust and try to be open with our supervisor. Again, bearing in mind that supervision involves management, education, support and mediation, we should identify what sort of responses we are looking for. In supervision we take responsibility for our performance and any issues in relation to organizational, legal, ethical and professional standards.

Both the supervisor and supervisee need to prepare for supervision, commit to making it work, be open to feedback and share responsibility for problem-solving. In a supervisory relationship there is a danger that both parties can collude, or either may have a tendency to justify, explain or defend. Collusion is often about the elephant in the room; no one has the courage to name the problem (often a person) who is causing stress or difficulties in the church or organization. Anytime we begin a sentence with 'But' we need to look at what we are saying and ask ourselves what we are doing.

Simon and Marie had established a church outreach project with the full support of the church. A new minister arrived on the scene who was unenthusiastic and unsupportive. It wasn't his vision and he felt the funds committed could better be used elsewhere. Instead of being honest about this, the project dwindled to almost nothing through prevarication and inertia. A frank supervision session could have saved a lot of pain and frustration.

Supervision contracts and covenants

Whether we draw up a supervision contract or covenant is largely down to personal preference and context. Contracts tend to focus more on responsibility, and covenants on relationship. There are several reasons why covenanting is a beneficial approach to supervision:

- It enables us to take charge of our own learning and development and stresses personal responsibility and self-determination.
- It builds trust between us and our supervisor as both work out how the relationship will function and commit ourselves to the process.
- It takes seriously our uniqueness as we can agree a covenant that relates to who we are and what we do rather than fitting into someone else's structure. (Pearson, 1995, pp. 51–3)

When drawing up a contract or covenant these are some of the areas that need to be discussed:

- *Purpose* What are the key areas that we need to cover and what will the balance of management, education, support (and possibly mediation) be? This might be broad brushstrokes over a year rather than for each session.

- *Confidentiality* Our usual guidelines for confidentiality are that it is not broken unless the individual or the people they are working with are at risk and even then we would usually inform the supervisee that this is what we are going to do. Confidentiality should be two-way in supervision; supervisees should assume that what is said or seen is confidential as well as the other way round. 'Guess what film the vicar's 12-year-old daughter was watching when I went round for supervision' is gossip and breaking trust although tempting for some to share. Always be aware of the relevant safeguarding or child protection policies in such discussions.

- *Practical details* How often will we meet and for how long? Where will supervision take place? Can we meet without interruption or distraction? What ground rules or boundaries do we want to have in place? What structure will the sessions have?

- *Commitment* Supervision should have a high priority with cancellations only happening for illness or an emergency and swiftly rearranged. Both parties need to prepare and expectations of this should be agreed. Agree who draws up the agenda, when it is circulated and what information, if any, is needed in advance.

- *Recording* What format of notes will be taken? Who will take them? Where will they be kept? Consider an action-points approach to recording, and email can be a simple way of making sure both parties have a copy.

- *Review* Agree when and how frequently supervision will be reviewed.

Although the content of supervision sessions will partly depend on context, there are some core areas that would usually be covered:

- agreeing an agenda or adding any items to the existing agenda;
- a general, open-ended question to start the conversation such as, 'How's it going?';
- updating from both parties on any information that either should know, particularly after time off;

- reviewing work since the last supervision session;
- planning the next period of work;
- determining priorities;
- any specific issues, difficulties or problems including people;
- any support, education or training needs;
- always ask if there is anything the supervisee wants to raise even if they didn't say anything when you agreed the agenda (many of us are familiar with the convention that the most important thing to be said is uttered as the person leaves the room at the end of a meeting);
- agree and note action points and anything else that needs recording and confirm or arrange the next meeting.

At the end of a supervision session a supervisee should feel valued, thoughtful, supported, clearer about their work and motivated (Ingram and Harris, 2001, p. 106). The challenge for the supervisor is how this is done; it will vary according to personality as different people tend to want to be praised and encouraged for different things depending on their own values.

Models of supervision

Most of us have a natural style of supervision and identified approaches in ministry include these (Beisswenger cited in Stevens, 1995, pp. 89–91):

- work evaluation mode, where the supervisor is in control and seeks to set the agenda;
- instructor mode, where the supervisor determines the learning needs of the supervisee;
- apprentice mode, where the supervisor sees the supervisee as learning from them and modelling various ministry skills and activities;
- training mode, where the supervisor seeks to establish an environment where the supervisee can grow and develop;
- resource mode, where the supervisor is there when needed by the supervisee but offers little in the way of direction;

- consultative mode, where the supervisor is there to facilitate the learning of the supervisee and offers support and anything else that is needed;
- spiritual guide mode, where the supervisor focuses on engaging in theological reflection and looking for meaning in the various ministry experiences the supervisee has.

Which of these we adopt will vary depending on our personality, that of the supervisee, levels of experience and roles undertaken. This list, along with the metaphors below, give an idea of the shades of meaning that are brought to the task of supervision and the role of supervisor. Realizing what our styles (or those of our supervisor) are can help us understand what is brought to the process, or we may identify styles or nuances that we want to add to our repertoire that are appropriate for different people.

Metaphors of supervision

Metaphors are a useful tool. 'The strength of metaphor lies in its potential to assist change through reflection on one's own practices, rather than through external prescription, which may meet resistance or mere compliance' (Mackinnon, 2004, p. 404). Although writing about academic supervision, Brockbank and McGill identify seven areas that have relevance to many other contexts: facilitator, teacher, assessor, counsellor, colleague, manager, advisor (1998, p. 237). When training youth workers in this field the overwhelming first choice of approach was that of facilitator, which is a positive mindset for supervision in collaborative ministry with its inferences of helping the individual rather than controlling them. Conroy offers these metaphors for supervisors in her context of spiritual direction supervision: companion, codiscerner, reverent evoker, contemplative presence, resting place, skilled helper and teacher (1995, p. 15). Again, you can see how the context influences the metaphors. In reflecting on our experience of collaborative ministry these are others we would offer: shelter, sustainer, encourager, builder, interpreter, process analyser, healer, coach, oracle, confessor, dream-holder, confidant, safety net, liberator, affirmer, bread-giver, absolver, comforter. Using this sort of language to talk about what you want from and bring to supervision can help draw out some of the fears, hopes and expectations of the process.

Group supervision

Within collaborative ministry it may be that group supervision would provide some benefits. Sometimes in group supervision an external facilitator is appointed, which may avoid the leader dominating or controlling. Before undertaking group supervision it needs to be clear what the boundaries are, particularly in terms of what can be agreed or changed through the process, otherwise it is frustrating for participants. A facilitator would usually agree ground rules at the beginning of the session, which would include confidentiality, time frame and the importance of working in an anti-oppressive way that respects all participants. Morrison (1996, p. 40) believes that group supervision has benefits that include:

- generation of more ideas and options;
- giving a wider view of perspectives;
- enabling the exploration of complex issues;
- providing a safe climate to work experientially in;
- generating a sense of corporate responsibility for problem-solving;
- facilitating peer learning;
- facilitating the giving and receiving of feedback in a supportive setting.

In a group setting it can be helpful if one or two people bring particular issues to explore, perhaps using some of the tools below.

Theological perspectives

Although you will not find the term supervision in the Bible, it can be seen as having biblical roots. Pohly (1993, pp. 9–10) identifies covenant as the underpinning biblical concept for supervision. He notes that God's covenant with Israel involved both promise and response: 'I will make of you a great nation' (Genesis 12.2), and 'you shall keep my covenant' (Genesis 19.9). He emphasizes that the new covenant that God makes (Jeremiah 31.29–34) is a life-centred model calling for mutual accountability, offering personal ownership, and being spiritually dynamic and life-giving (1993, pp. 102–3). He suggests that we approach supervision with this as a foundation and prefers the term covenant to the more often used contract. He notes that the pattern established in the New Testament of bishops, deacons and elders (1 Timothy) involves supervisory functions, and that Christ is presented as a shepherd and guardian of souls (1 Peter 2.25).

The Bible offers much advice about how we should treat one another; these points seem particularly pertinent for supervision:

- Love one another (John 13.34).
- Accept one another (Romans 15.7).
- Be compassionate to one another (Ephesians 4.32).
- Serve one another (1 Peter 4.10).
- Bear one another's burdens (Galatians 6.2).
- Pray for one another (James 5.16).
- Forgive one another (Ephesians 4.32).
- Do not speak against one another (James 5.9).
- Be at peace with one another (Mark 9.50).

One of the difficulties with supervision from a theological perspective is that some have what they believe to be a biblical understanding and take it to an extreme which leads to what has been called 'heavy shepherding' where individuals are not given autonomy and are expected to be highly accountable to a particular leader. Collaborative ministry will not work with this approach to supervision as it mitigates against an every-member ministry attitude and establishes a hierarchical model where people don't have the opportunity to exercise their gifts in an appropriate way.

Issues and problems in supervision

Supervision is not a stress-free activity and in both parties there may be anxieties about the process. Both supervisors and supervisees may fear rejection and both may act in a way that they think the other wants or in a way that means they will be more liked. Some supervisors will think that they need to have all the answers and worry when they don't, particularly when others treat them as though they should. Conversely, supervisees can fear that their limitations will be exposed when asked questions or if they disclose something that has not gone as well as it might have done. A number of our youth work students have commented on how they were encouraged to share a pastoral issue in supervision which was later held against them. When people from different disciplines are supervising each other there can be concerns from either party that their methods, approaches or attitudes may be challenged because of the alternative perspective of the other. An issue for some supervisees is that supervision challenges their autonomy and independence and, in a Christian context, their capacity (as they see it) to follow the Holy Spirit's leading rather than being held back by a boss who doesn't understand.

Personality impacts interpersonal exchanges and supervision is no exception. Many of us will resonate with one or more of these beliefs (Claxton cited by Morrison, 1996, p. 33):

• I must be competent.
• I must be in control.
• I must be consistent.
• I must be comfortable.

The difficulty of supervision is that it is likely that there will be times when either the supervisor or the supervisee identifies areas of incompetence, inconsistency and discomfort that impact our ability to be in control. Good covenants or contracts may help but honesty and vulnerability when such situations arise is likely to be the most effective remedy. Knowing what our predisposition is at least means we can look out for our baggage when it emerges.

Authority can be an issue in ministry supervision. In a managerial supervisory relationship, authority is usually clear; within collaborative ministry it is usually a little fuzzy as often boundaries of authority have not been clearly articulated within a church or ministry setting. Within a straightforward employment context, supervision involves accountability to the vision and objectives of the organization and to agreed performance standards, and a deficiency in any of these would need to be addressed. We may want to be able to do this in ministry too but this needs expectations to be explicit and the conditions for joining a collaborative ministry team spelt out. Too often we are so desperate for volunteers that we take who we can get and live with the consequences. Chapter 6 on teamwork can help address some of these issues.

Making supervision work

These are tips we have learnt from our experience:

• Invest in the relationship at the beginning and give adequate time to getting to know each other and working out the best way to work together.

- Build trust and respect, and value each other's roles and expect to learn from each other.
- Realize any one supervisor can't meet all our needs.
- Be clear about expectations on both sides including both people following through on actions and decisions.
- Look at learning from mistakes rather than attaching blame.
- Have clear boundaries particularly if our manager helps with an area of our work.
- Learn how to give and receive feedback and don't default to being defensive.
- Don't collude in avoiding conflict if both of you have that tendency, work out ways of identifying and dealing with it.
- Adopt the I'm OK, you're OK mentality, when one of you doesn't feel OK see why and what you can do about it.
- Be committed to win–win as a philosophy.
- Use tools such as MBTI, Belbin or Enneagram to explore how each other works. Tools like this don't box but give a shared vocabulary to explore issues in a less threatening way.
- Review, evaluate and reflect regularly.

Tools for supervision

Sometimes it helps to have something specific to discuss as part of a supervision meeting as well as it being beneficial for the supervisee to be undertaking some systematic reflection on what they do. These are some of the tools that can be used.

Supervisory conversation (Pohly, 1993, pp. 83–4)

1 *Informative stage* The focus is on getting an accurate picture of the event or situation:
   What took place? What was the situation?
   What was your role?
   How did you respond?
   Who were the other participants? How did you interact with them?
   How is this related to other events or situations?
   How typical is it? Is it part of a pattern?
   How does the situation stand now? Is there unfinished business?

2 *Evaluation stage* The focus is on the core issue(s) so as to sort out what the real problem is and/or what needs attention first:
What emotions did you experience?
What are your feelings about it now?
How do you feel about the other people involved?
How do you feel about your place of ministry? About what you are doing?
In what way are or are not your expectations being fulfilled?
How does this event or situation correspond with others in your life?
What would you do differently if you could?
How does all this affect your ability to minister?
What are the key issues for you?
What is the most important?

3 *Analysis* The focus is on removing the obstacles and finding among alternative possibilities the one that seems most viable for continued ministry in the situation:
What do you want to have happen? In supervision? In the situation?
What is your interpretation of the situation now?
What would you change? What would that require?
What do you see as alternatives?
What would happen if . . . ?
What is your role as a result of the experience?
How can the continuing situation best be confronted or handled?

4 *Theologizing stage* The focus is on meanings so as to draw from this experience and prior or new knowledge those elements that now become 'truth' in the light of the gospel:
What have you learned from this experience?
What new insights do you have about self, human nature, Church, world, God?
At what points does your experience intersect with the Christian gospel? In what ways?
What does this have to say to you about ministry?
What are the implications for yourself as a minister? Weaknesses? Strengths?
How do you feel about ministry? About yourself in ministry?
What emerges as the ultimate concern for you?

5 *Commitment stage* The focus is on decision in terms of choosing a ministering response:

How is this situation like those you anticipate in the future?

How do you anticipate responding to them?

What are you going to do about the situation brought for supervision?

What is your next step?

What resources do you need?

What faith response (action) must and will you make as a Christian as a result of this decision?

Case studies

Case studies are another way of using supervision time to reflect on ministry. This model is adapted from Pyle and Seals (1995, pp. 101–2). Case studies need to be well prepared to be used effectively and can be presented just verbally or through a written summary that can be read in advance.

For example, you may talk about a recent visit you made to someone whose husband has just been diagnosed with dementia, and how you found it hard to answer her questions about why God lets things like this happen and what had she done to deserve this. You left feeling inadequate and that you hadn't met her expectations of a visit from the pastoral team. It also made you think about your mum's last months in a care home and how she cried each time you left, and you realized you still haven't really dealt with the guilt you felt about not looking after her at home. Or Jez is your gap-year student and you are managing his programme but are responsible to the minister for him. One of the parents has come to you and said that she thinks he is a bad influence because he invited her son and a couple of his mates back to the church flat to play *Grand Theft Auto* (a violent video game). All the lads were over 18 and it was in Jez's own time, and you are not sure what to do.

1 *Introduction* State the dilemma and any decision that needs to be made and give an indication as to some of the possibilities for those involved.

2 *Background* Set the context including any necessary background information about people or events. Try to be objective and avoid value judgements.

3 *Development* Give a chronological account as well as identifying and analysing the main issues. Include everything relevant to the dilemma and the decision that needs to be made.

4 *Summary* Answer the question: 'What should I do now?'

Creative approaches

Activities that you use in other contexts may be useful in supervision (see Lahad, 2000, for lots of ideas). A more creative approach can sometimes access feelings or insights that do not come when just talking. For example, we often use art-based activities to aid reflection and these can be used near the beginning of the session to begin a discussion on where the supervisee is at, what they are feeling, etc. This may include using clay, using colour, using lines, shapes and squiggles, for example. Letter-writing (when letters are not sent) or imaginary dialogues can help resolve issues or ensure that all the issues have been brought out into the open. Guided journeys or Ignatian contemplation exercises (where an individual puts themselves into a Bible story that resonates with where they are at) are other tools that can be used. Sometimes a poem, song or a film clip can be used to start a conversation about a difficult topic. When doing anything different in supervision it is usually good to get agreement and not to impose activities on someone who is clearly unwilling. There are also ideas in other chapters that may be useful in the context of supervision too.

Points for reflection, discussion and action

- What are your perspectives on supervision?
- What baggage do you bring to the process? How does that impact your participation?
- How might supervision be beneficial in your context?
- Is covenant or contract the more appropriate approach? Why?
- What metaphor or model of supervision resonates with you? Can you think of one more apt for your context?
- In what ways would group supervision be beneficial in your context?
- Which of the ideas on making supervision work do you need to adopt?

8

Conflict skills

> [Humankind] must evolve for all human conflict a method which rejects
> revenge, aggression, and retaliation.   (Martin Luther King, Jr)

Conflict is a fact of life. Throughout our lives we face different kinds
of conflict, and our response to these situations will vary depending
on our personality, upbringing, situation, mood and various other
factors. We have observed in Christian settings, and especially
churches, people are generally fearful of conflict, perhaps because
the stakes can appear particularly high relationally. The Chinese
characters that form the word 'crisis' are those representing danger
and opportunity. This seems relevant as we explore how issues
around conflict relate to collaborative ministry. Conflict can often
appear and feel destructive, but it is not necessarily so. It can provide opportunities for growth, development and creativity. However,
many of us are not good at dealing creatively and constructively
with conflict, and when conflict is tackled inappropriately, or, worse
perhaps, ignored or repressed, it can be very damaging.

Whenever we are working with others we will inevitably encounter some kind of conflict. Thompson (2006, p. 5) suggests:

> A common mistake is for people to assume that conflict is what
> occurs when relationships break down. However, in reality, relation-
> ships can be characterized by conflict over a very long period of time
> without ever breaking down. Conflict, or at least the potential for
> conflict, is present in all relationships.

In any ministry setting, conflict skills form an essential part of the
toolkit required.

Many different types of conflict arise in collaborative ministry contexts. These include:

- *Goal conflict* Focusing around mission, vision, aims, objectives and
  goals.

- *Role conflict* Focusing around the tension between different roles we might have.
- *Cognitive conflict* Focusing around ideas, opinions, values, judgements and ways of thinking.
- *Affective conflict* Focusing around feelings, emotions and responses.
- *Relational conflict* Focusing around communication and relationships with others.
- *Behavioural conflict* Focusing around values, words, actions and behaviour.
- *Spiritual conflict* Focusing around issues of spirituality and religion.
- *Self-conflict* Focusing around inner struggles and tensions.

Sources of conflict

Conflict usually arises when differences cannot be satisfactorily dealt with. Adirondack (1996, p. 136) asserts that differences become conflict if:

- People are unwilling to accept the validity of differing values, priorities or views of what is 'right' or 'important'.
- Individuals have different or unclear standards for action, behaviour or performance and cannot agree common standards.
- Something (money, attention, work, responsibility) is, or is perceived to be, unfairly distributed.
- People feel an individual or collective need to win, be right, get their own way or dominate.
- People fear, distrust and define anyone different or unknown as 'other', 'outsider' or 'enemy'.
- People do not want to change.
- There are unclear or non-existent procedures for discussing and resolving differences before they escalate.

As we will explore further in the next chapter, we need to recognize and value difference as an essential part of life.

Theological perspectives

One of the things which often makes it difficult to value and engage with conflict in Christian contexts is the way the concept of unity is interpreted and emphasized in some settings. The impression given can be that agreement with others is essential, that conformity with existing norms is evidence of spiritual maturity and uniformity far preferable to diversity.

The opening verse of Psalm 133 is often used to paint a picture of an ideal world, where all is well between believers. 'How very good and pleasant it is when kindred live together in unity!' (Psalm 133.1). This image, in a Song of Ascents, pictures the arrival of pilgrims to Jerusalem and uses metaphors of priestly oil (verse 2) and refreshing dew (verse 3) to emphasize the blessings that unity can bring.

In the New Testament there is also a call to the early Church to nurture their relationships, 'making every effort to maintain the unity of the Spirit in the bond of peace' (Ephesians 4.3). This is the only time the Greek word *henotes* – unity or oneness – is used specifically. It is worth noting that the word is used in the context of working towards and for unity, rather than expecting an automatic sense of oneness to be present. Jesus' prayer in John 17 shows his desire to see the disciples experiencing the kind of relational harmony he knows with his Father:

> As you, Father, are in me and I am in you, may they also be in us, so that the world may believe that you have sent me. The glory that you have given me I have given them, so that they may be one, as we are one, I in them and you in me, that they may become completely one.
> (John 17.21–23)

Again, it appears here and in other passages (Ephesians 2.19–22; 4.14–16; Colossians 3.14–16) that unity is about process, working through issues, growing together into togetherness and mutuality, rather than about simple blind agreement or sameness. Conflict inevitably will be part of this process, and can potentially bring about greater unity in the long term.

Personal responses to conflict

> First keep the peace within yourself, then you can also bring peace to others.
> (Thomas à Kempis)

Developing self-awareness involves becoming aware of underlying factors which underpin our personal responses to conflict. Understanding our reactions – whether physical, mental, emotional or spiritual – should help us manage conflict more effectively and equip us to discover approaches and tools which suit us best. Socialization helps in understanding group dynamics but is equally significant in considering personal responses to conflict. Our upbringing will probably influence us strongly. As we grow we learn to respond in particular ways, depending on what proves effective. Our parents or carers often influence us by modelling certain ways of behaving so if we never see anger expressed healthily in childhood we may grow up fearful of anger or believing it to be wrong. Other influential role models might include close friends, teachers, colleagues at work and church leaders.

Learning to understand our personality type can be helpful here too. Our personality is likely to influence whether we tend to remain calm in stressful situations, whether we are anxious, impulsive, impatient or irritable. Cultural factors can also play a part. Assumptions around gender roles can lead to men and women being expected to respond in particular ways. One common stereotype is that women tend not to be angry but express other emotions, while for men anger is more acceptable, other emotions less so. Broader racial or cultural issues may impact too and certain organizations will have expectations – either explicit or implicit – regarding what is seen as acceptable.

Mental models

Mental models are 'deeply held internal images of how the world works, images that limit us to familiar ways of thinking and acting' (Senge, 2006, p. 163). We all carry mental models of how people will see us and respond to us and we generally expect them to behave in that way. Our mental models contribute to conflict because they prevent us seeing and hearing what is actually happening – rather, we become blinded by our own preconceived ideas about people or situations.

Mike's job was demanding at the best of times, but was requiring him to work late most evenings. This meant he ended up missing two consecutive elders' meetings. He was aware the other elders never missed a meeting and felt guilty about his absence. He could imagine the conversations about his lack of commitment and skewed priorities. He arrived late to the meeting following this, waiting for the barbed comments and criticism and when Barbara asked him if he'd had a tough day at work he felt himself bristling inwardly. It was obviously her way of having a 'dig'. Part-way through the meeting the group offered to pray for Mike and, still fuming, he grudgingly agreed. The prayers which followed almost brought him to tears. They expressed loving care for him personally and demonstrated insight into his complex work situations. Mike's mental models had caused him to see and hear criticism where there was none and the meeting could easily have had a different outcome had Mike's thinking not been challenged and changed by the prayer time.

Self-fulfilling prophecies are closely connected to mental models and begin with someone being labelled. This can happen as part of group dynamics, through childhood experiences or in adult contexts. If people or groups are consistently labelled they will often begin to live up to that label. This can contribute to the escalation of conflict and prevent some approaches to resolving conflict from working effectively.

Defence mechanisms

As individuals, some of our own preferred responses to conflict situations may demonstrate an assertive and mature attitude. In other cases, we will adopt what is commonly known as a 'defence mechanism' to cope with our anxiety.

- *Avoidance or 'flight'* involves avoiding conflict by ignoring the situation completely or pretending it isn't happening, avoiding an individual or group or simply acquiescing in situations where we feel under pressure. Some people will use humour as a flight mechanism – making a joke instead of addressing the issue. Rescuing behaviour is also a form of flight.
- *Attack or 'fight'* can manifest in aggressive or defensive comments, bullying or using power, intellect or position to put someone down. 'Attack is the best form of defence' is the underlying principle for this kind of response.
- *Dependency* looks to someone else for rescue, by appealing for help, adopting a 'victim' mentality, looking to a key person or leader to assist or recruiting support within or outside of a group. Dependency avoids taking responsibility in conflict.

Group-level defences

Defence mechanisms operate on a personal level but also become ingrained in groups and teams as norms. When this happens we have what Bion describes as group-level 'basic assumption'. These are unconscious processes where the group colludes to preserve the unity of the group at all costs (Bion, 1961). At a group level, defence mechanisms are magnified. So, for example, a dependent group will focus on the leader for their sense of security and place little value on other members' contributions. When group-level defences operate, individuals tend to subordinate their normal personal responses to that of the group as a whole. Normally assertive individuals might suddenly demonstrate flight mentality, because of unconscious pressure within the group. As with other unconscious processes, there are no simple answers for tackling group-level defence mechanisms, but employing good facilitation skills, seeking to maintain emotional distance from the group and seeking discernment and wisdom can be beneficial.

Approaching conflict situations

The basic skills we have highlighted throughout this book are foundational when it comes to conflict skills and should assist us in developing our own approaches and styles. Facilitation skills are of particular value, highlighting the importance of communication, respect, shared responsibility and participation, creating space for listening, reflection and exploration. We believe certain other principles will also underpin our approaches to conflict effectively.

Being proactive

> You can't stay in your corner of the forest waiting for others to come to you. You have to go to them sometimes. (A. A. Milne, *Winnie the Pooh*)

Choosing to be proactive in conflict situations ensures we don't go into 'flight' mode. Sometimes it will be appropriate to let an emotionally charged moment pass before responding, but generally it is better to address conflict or potential conflict before it can escalate. This often means taking the initiative, particularly where others are reluctant to address issues.

Avoiding 'extreme' reactions

In conflict, we can sometimes find ourselves responding in extreme ways. If a situation has been causing stress for some time, we can be tempted to let off steam by lumping numerous issues together. It is important to try and tackle the issue at hand, rather than expressing many complaints, which will leave others feeling attacked and encourage defensive responses. Extreme reactions may also occur if the situation touches deeper issues within our history or experience. In our responses, as well as seeking to avoid overreaction, we should try to steer clear of sweeping generalizations, for example, using words like 'never' ('You never listen to me!') and 'always' ('You always do that!').

Seeking first to understand

Covey (1989, p. 237) identifies the importance of seeking first to understand and then to be understood as key to good relationships and handling difficult issues. Attentive and active listening will assist this process. We can all interpret someone's words through the filter of our own preconceived ideas, mental models, values, opinions and assumptions and it is incredibly helpful to take time to ensure that we really have understood what the other person is seeking to communicate.

Actions speak louder

It has been suggested that as little as 7 per cent of a conversation is transmitted by what is said, while 38 per cent is transmitted by how it is said and 55 per cent is transmitted by other non-verbal language (Barnes, 2002, p. 27). In conflict it is important to be aware of our body language and to seek to avoid defensiveness (folded arms), nervousness (fidgeting), anger (pursed lips, clenched fists) or aggressive stances (hands on hips, chin jutting out, towering over people).

Remembering our values

In the heat of the moment or the pain of disappointment, hurt or betrayal our values can sometimes go out of the window. In conflict it is vital to pause and remember the foundation on which we are seeking to build our lives. Unfortunately, grace and love are often used as excuses for flight behaviour, but responding in a godly manner does not mean avoiding conflict, particularly if we then go and rehearse our grievances with others. We need to prayerfully consider how values like love, grace, forgiveness, integrity, peace and joy will inform and influence our responses. An attitude of humility will not necessarily assume we are wrong and the other person is right, but will ensure we approach the situation willing to listen and learn.

Being aware

We have emphasized the importance of self-awareness throughout this book and it is just as valuable here. Personally, we need to ensure we stay open to feedback and criticism, own our feelings and opinions and avoid bullying, manipulation, misusing power or inappropriate humour. Having honest friends who give us feedback about our own attitudes and behaviour is essential.

It is also important not to over-spiritualize conflict situations. Much conflict may have a spiritual dynamic and prayer is important. However, we need to look at the spiritual dynamic as part of the picture, rather than the whole and we must avoid jumping to over-spiritualized conclusions which label, accuse or demonize others.

Learning and growing

'We know that all things work together for good for those who love God' (Romans 8.28) encourages us to understand how God can use every situation for our good. Our approaches and responses to conflict will be significantly impacted if we believe and understand that every situation in life, however painful, can contribute to our learning and growth. This is not a shallow platitude but a principle we have sought to implement and outwork in our own lives and which we have found incredibly beneficial. For example, consciously pausing to ask ourselves the question, 'What can I learn from this?' can help us draw out discoveries about ourselves, others, God and the world around us. Using some of the reflective practice skills we outlined in Chapter 4 can give a helpful framework to this process.

Needs, interests and positions

Choose your battles wisely . . . life is filled with opportunities to choose between making a big deal out of something or simply letting it go, realising it doesn't really matter. If you choose your battles wisely, you'll be far more effective in winning those that are truly important.

(Carlson, 1997, p. 77)

Fisher *et al.* (2000, p. 27) have developed an onion-like model to explore the difference between needs, interests and positions. In the centre are our needs – what we must have. Further out are layers of interests – what we really want. On the outermost layers are our positions – what we say we want. Interestingly, someone's positions might differ significantly from their interests and needs, meaning their behaviour might not reflect what's really going on inside. It is useful to identify and clarify each of these different areas for all those involved in a conflict situation.

Needs

Conflict can arise from people's real or perceived needs (see Adair, 1983, p. 36). Maslow identified various needs and asserted that they are a hierarchy with one level of need having to be met before an individual was able to focus on a higher level.

- *Physiological* Food, water, sleep.
- *Safety* Security, protection from danger.
- *Social* Belonging, acceptance, social life, friendship, love.
- *Esteem* Self-respect, achievement, status recognition.
- *Self-actualization* Growth, accomplishment, personal development.

For example, if a team member is feeling threatened by a change in group structure and dynamic (safety need), it will be unhelpful to focus on self-esteem issues. What they really need is to feel secure in the group. Seeking to identify accurately the needs of the individuals or groups involved is therefore an important starting point, but can be a challenge. Being open about our needs puts us in a vulnerable place and people will often mask their real needs with a different issue.

Interests

When seeking to identify interests it is important to listen carefully and avoid assumptions. Checking out with the person or people involved what they are really thinking or feeling is essential if we are to get a more accurate picture of what is really happening. We must avoiding attacking or accusatory language here as this is likely to lead to defensiveness or justification. Showing that we understand and value someone's interests is important here.

Conflict skills

Positions

People will adopt positions in a conflict situation for all kinds of reasons. Sometimes they might genuinely feel strongly about the issue and their position will be a real one. At other times they might adopt a position to mask a real need or interest, to make a point, out of sympathy for a friend or colleague or because of an underlying resentment towards someone else. Some people just enjoy playing devil's advocate and don't have any real commitment to a position they argue.

Helpful ways forward

It is least helpful to address conflict at the positions level because as soon as people take up positions they risk losing face if they are then asked to give them up. Instead, if possible it is helpful to seek to reconnect with the real interests and needs behind the position. This will call for careful listening and openness. When approaching positions, interests and needs we need to focus on the problem and avoid any kind of personal attacks or criticism wherever possible.

Skills for responding to conflict

There are many different levels of conflict and in many cases it is possible to diffuse conflict before it escalates through conversation, simple listening and by using some of the approaches we have already highlighted. Addressing 'low-level' conflict before it intensifies is obviously preferable to allowing issues to spiral out of hand. However, at times we are likely to find ourselves facing situations where conflict has already escalated and more specific skills and tools are required.

Mediation

Mediation is a way of helping those who are in conflict to resolve their differences by talking to each other. It involves mediators, people who are trained to listen to those in conflict and to help them resolve their disagreements. They facilitate reconciliation by creating space and a supportive framework within which those in disagreement can resolve the problem themselves, and so take ownership of their situation.

(Macbeth and Fine, 1995, p. 147)

117

Mediation processes can be particularly helpful where a significant breakdown in relationship makes communication difficult. The presence of a third party, who has no personal agenda, can create safe space for exploration. Mediators work facilitatively, setting and maintaining boundaries, agreeing ground rules and encouraging mutual listening. They do not carry authority in the situation, do not give advice or judge and seek to remain impartial throughout. A mediation process can involve (Macbeth and Fine, 1995, p. 152):

- *Opening* Welcome, setting boundaries and ground rules.
- *Listening to what happened* Each party summarizes the situation.
- *Stating what each person wants* Mediator asks questions to clarify and summarizes.
- *Fiding solutions* Establishing what each party is willing to do and finding solutions that are realistic, specific and balanced.
- *Agreeing* Reviewing and confirming points of agreement.
- *Closing statement* Affirmation, conclusion, thanks.

Mediators may also be involved in following up the process, monitoring how things go or evaluating, although this is not always the case.

Advocacy

Advocacy involves intervening or negotiating on behalf of one party. This differs from conciliation and mediation where those facilitating are expected to remain unbiased. An advocate can legitimately seek to put across the views and standpoints of one party in a conflict.

Negotiation

Negotiation involves discussing each party's needs, demands and interests and agreeing which aspects of each should be incorporated into a solution. Processes of negotiation will require those involved to be willing to compromise even if they start with very different objectives. Without a willingness to move from established positions, negotiation will be fruitless. The aim in negotiation is to find an outcome in which both parties feel satisfied. Macbeth and Fine highlight possible stages in a negotiation process (1995, p. 144):

- *Preparation* Clarifying what is wanted.
- *Discussion* Each side stating their position.

- *Proposing* Movement begins as suggestions are made ('What if . . . then perhaps').
- *Bargaining* Parties begin to move towards each other through 'give and take'.
- *Agreeing* Parties come to an agreement. It may be helpful for this to be put in writing.

Assertiveness skills

Assertiveness focuses on identifying our responses to situations in terms of whether we respond passively, aggressively, passive-aggressively or assertively. Briefly summarized, these responses are as follows:

Passive

Someone responding passively is likely to adopt 'flight' behaviour and will often retreat from conflict, hide their feelings and avoid confrontation. They will tend to assume that they have the problem, not the other person ('I'm not OK, you're OK') and may tend towards a victim or martyr mentality. In conflict they will often sacrifice their own desires for the sake of peace ('I lose, you win').

Aggressive

Someone responding aggressively is more likely to adopt 'fight' behaviour, attacking verbally, dominating or bullying. They will often see conflict as a power struggle and assume the other person is in the wrong ('I'm OK, you're not OK'). They are likely to be blunt, competitive and keen to get their way at all costs ('I win, you lose').

Passive-aggressive

Someone responding passive-aggressively may look passive, but there is a sting in the tail of their behaviour. They will hide their feelings and avoid direct confrontation, but will often manipulate, undermine or recruit support to try and get their own way. Their negative attitude is focused both internally and externally ('I'm not OK, you're not OK') and they may make snide remarks or spoil things for everyone ('I lose, you lose').

Assertive

Someone responding assertively will adopt neither flight nor fight behaviour but will face issues and seek resolution. They will be accepting of themselves and others ('I'm OK, you're OK') and be aware of their own feelings, expressing these honestly and calmly. They will seek a way forward which brings about a positive outcome for all those involved ('I win, you win' or 'win–win').

Assertiveness involves being aware of and considerate of our own needs.

> Unless I both value myself, and have the sense that some other people value me for at least some of the time, I am not likely to function very well. I shall neither feel very loving to myself or to anyone else. Which is bad news for the people I meet. So having a realistic sense of my value is not egocentric. It is socially useful.
>
> (Houston, 1984, p. 34)

This will include recognizing that our opinions, feelings and needs are as important as anyone else's and that it is OK for us to be ourselves, question, disagree, express opinions, struggle and make mistakes. Part of this is accepting that we are not going to please everyone all the time.

A helpful tool emerging from assertiveness approaches is the concept of 'I' statements. An 'I' statement is a way of clearly expressing a point of view about a situation. It involves describing how the situation is affecting us and what we would like to see change. It is not accusatory and carries no expectations (Macbeth and Fine, 1995, p. 82). It encourages the individual concerned to take responsibility and 'own' their own responses and feelings and is structured in three parts.

The first part summarizes the situation in a factual statement, expressed as objectively and clearly as possible ('When . . .'). The second part expresses how the individual feels without blaming or accusing ('I feel . . .'). The third part states the preferred change or outcome, without demanding or pressurizing ('What I would like is . . .'). Some examples of 'I' statements in a collaborative ministry context would include the following.

When annoyed with someone arriving consistently late to meetings: 'When you arrive late I feel awkward because I don't want to start without you. What I would like is for you to try and set off a bit earlier so that you get here on time.'

When frustrated by someone texting during a team meeting: 'When you use your mobile during team meetings I feel frustrated because I find it distracting, and what I would really like is for you to text during the breaks and switch your phone off at other times.'

When seeking to encourage a quiet team member to contribute: 'When you don't contribute to our discussions I feel sad because I feel we're missing out on all you have to offer and I would really like to hear what you have to say about the issues we're discussing.'

In reflecting on appropriate approaches to difficult situations, Thompson (2006, pp. 65–6) describes the concept of 'elegant challenging'. 'Elegant means sophisticated, and so an elegant challenge is one that is not crude or ill-thought through. It is where the person doing the challenging raises the issue in a helpful way, rather than an aggressive or attacking way.'

Tools for responding to conflict

Mapping a conflict

A helpful approach in responding to conflict is to map it out. There are different ways of doing this. One is to use a mind map (Buzan, 2005). This involves starting in the centre of a piece of paper with a key word or phrase representing the conflict and then allowing thoughts and ideas to connect to these. Each of these thoughts and ideas should be connected using 'branches', with colours and images used throughout. Mind maps can be very simple or highly intricate. Examples can be found on <www.buzanworld.com>.

Another mapping approach is adapted from Mediation at Work <www.mediationatwork.com>.

- Identify the issue, problem or situation in a single phrase or sentence and put this in the centre of a sheet of paper, without seeking to focus on or analyse the nature of the problem.
- Identify the main individuals or groups of people involved and write their names around the central situation.
- Identify the potential needs and fears of each individual or group involved and write these next to their names.
- Identify new learning and insights, complementary needs and fears across the map, common ground and potentially hidden agendas. Seek to imagine what it might be like to be in the place of each person or group. Look for new insights, areas of difficulty

which need most attention and seek to create options for moving forward.

Circles of concern and influence

This was developed by Stephen Covey (1989) as a means of developing self-awareness and proactivity. On a piece of paper we draw two circles, one larger and one smaller, the smaller should be inside the larger one. In the outer circle – the circle of concern – we write all the things we are concerned about in the conflict situation. As we reflect it will become evident that we have no control over some of these things. There will be other things that we can actually do something about. These should be written in the smaller circle, the circle of influence – our attitudes and responses fall in this circle, for example. Focusing our attention on our circle of concern will lead to anxiety and frustration. These are areas for prayer rather than action. However, focusing our attention on our circle of influence, on things we can affect or change, will encourage us to take responsibility, be proactive and often begins to affect things in the outer circle.

Six thinking hats

Edward de Bono's 'six thinking hats' technique (De Bono, 2000) can be used alone or in meetings to look at problems in different ways. Each hat represents a different style of thinking and by 'putting on' different hats, we can intentionally engage with alternative ways of approaching situations. This can be done alone by putting on each coloured hat in turn to see things in each different way, or by each person in the group adopting a different coloured hat and representing that particular perspective.

- *White hat* Focuses on data and information and seeks to analyse this.
- *Red hat* Engages with intuition, emotion and gut reaction.
- *Black hat* Takes a deliberately negative view, seeking to identify drawbacks and weaknesses.
- *Yellow hat* Chooses an optimistic perspective, highlighting benefits, advantages and positives.
- *Green hat* Develops creative, innovative solutions and allows 'out of the box' thinking.

- *Blue hat* Takes responsibility for process, chairs discussion and steers the thinking where needed.

Surviving conflict

Interpersonal conflict can be highly stressful. Where possible, it is important to avoid getting things out of perspective. One helpful question to ask is how the situation will look to us in a year's time. Rehearsing situations and/or possible conversations in our minds can be a common habit, but will often increase our anxiety. Because we respond to conflict in different ways, it is helpful to identify personal strategies for reducing stress. These may include ensuring a healthy work–life balance, having trusted people we can talk through issues with, knowing which leisure activities help us relax and unwind and seeking to draw learning and development from every situation we find ourselves in.

Points for reflection, discussion and action

- Think about your upbringing and what was communicated to you about conflict. How might this have affected the way you see conflict today?
- What defence mechanisms or habitual ways of responding can you identify in your own response to conflict situations?
- How easy do you find it to separate the people from the problem in conflict situations?
- Who are the people you can talk to in difficult times – who won't always agree, but will give wise counsel?
- What personal strategies can you identify that will help you cope better with conflict?

9

Diversity skills

A young man was on placement as a Youth for Christ volunteer at an Anglican church; he and the vicar became embroiled in a conversation about baptism. His parting shot to the vicar was, 'You do it your way, I'll do it God's.' Not the attitude to enhance collaborative ministry! With an increasing emphasis on collaborative ministry and interagency or multiagency work, having the skills and understanding to work with people who are different is vital. Working with people or organizations who are different from us may be harder work to begin with but often the end result is richer as we learn from those with diverse perspectives and often have a more holistic or realistic view as we move beyond our natural frame of reference. We also need to acknowledge that we sometimes shy away from working with others who are different because of fear, our stereotypes, concern about what others would think, unwillingness to make perceived compromises and so on. People with disabilities will occasionally say how some people tend to avoid them because they do not know how to relate to them; they are frightened of making a mistake. Political correctness has made many of us quite apprehensive about saying the wrong thing or acting in an oppressive way.

Principles

In seeking to value diversity there are certain principles that we believe are important to consider. The first is that we are all made in the image of God and we should seek to see and hear God in and through each other. Another is an acknowledgement that there are benefits to working in a multi-faith context as that is better for the profile and position of Christianity and certainly in Paul's hospital context it results in less marginalization and opens up opportunities

to understand what pastoral, spiritual and religious care means in contemporary culture. Having the right attitude is a crucial starting point:

> Reflection on the sacred dimension of life, on our own life and others'
> reminds us of some obligations we have. We must be wise in our care
> for ourselves and others and especially discerning in the face of any
> problems. When something seems to be wrong, we must take care to
> discover what it is and to find remedy for it. When there are oppor-
> tunities for enhancing or enriching others' lives, we must respect who
> they are and work in partnership with them. We must also take care
> to employ any resources required, including time, in a responsible way.
> (Fitchett, 2002, pp. 22–3)

In some contexts working with those who are different takes courage
and may well be risky. There may be historical and other reasons why
x does not work with y. To change this situation may take patience,
perseverance and tenacity but in the end may lead to a powerful statement that helps build the kingdom of God. A good place to begin is
always to see where we agree and build from there. This can begin
to build trust, understanding and appreciation. A starting place for
interfaith work can be the golden rule which is a common thread in
many faiths but is also a principle that those with no religious faith
can affirm too. It can be summarized as 'do to others as you would
have them do to you' (Luke 6.31).

Inclusiveness

In many ways diversity skill is as much, if not more, about attitude
than skill. A fundamental attitude is that of inclusivity. Do we really
believe in being inclusive? If so, to what degree? Have we thought
through why we do meetings at particular times, who we ask to help
with the children's work, that a single person may have family
responsibilities even though theirs are not as obvious as the couple's
with three young children? As we write this there is debate about
the 'Mosquito' – a device that makes a loud buzzing noise that
can be heard only by children and youths – being used in shopping
precincts to keep young people away. Do we have the equivalent
in our context that keeps a particular group or even individual
excluded from our community?

Anti-oppressive practice

In the caring professions anti-oppressive practice is an underpinning concept for practitioners. It has perhaps not always been part of the thinking in ministerial contexts but the idea is one that needs to be grappled with to work effectively with others who are different in a way that is respectful and empowering. All too often we can behave in ways that are disrespectful or offensive towards others but not necessarily realize this at the time. For example, a man greeting a woman of the opposite sex from some faith groups shouldn't shake hands, let alone offer a kiss, but in some European cultures not to offer a kiss would be unusual.

Thompson (1998, pp. 12–19) introduces the idea of a personal cultural structural (PCS) analysis as a way of understanding different layers of oppression. In collaborative ministry it is worth reflecting on whether oppression is happening at any of these levels as sometimes it is present but ignored or accepted as part of the culture. At a personal level the thoughts, feelings and actions of an individual impact others, which may result in prejudice and discrimination, particularly where that individual is in a position of power. As individuals we frequently form opinions of others or hold stereotypes which affect our behaviour. We need to be alert to our own personal prejudices, challenge them and try to ensure that our treatment of others is fair and unbiased. In a ministry context this may mean taking risks with people because they don't fit our preconceived ideas of who should take on a particular role. In some churches that is about age, in others class or perhaps gender, ethnicity or disability.

For example, Andy really wanted to be involved in ministry with young people but responses to his blindness had discouraged him from pursuing this so instead he applied for an administrative job with Youth for Christ. Sally saw his potential at interview and he was one of the first people to go through an apprenticeship scheme in Youth for Christ and now runs his own project with a focus on schools work <www.rolltherock.org.uk>.

Culture has an impact on all of us and shapes our values and norms. We often make cultural assumptions that we are not even necessarily aware of about particular groups or activities. Indeed, a lot of oppression is based on beliefs about the superiority of one group over another – racism, sexism, ageism, for example. This can lead to a lack of understanding of people from a different cultural back-ground and a characterizing of their norms and behaviour as negatively different or even abnormal. This story makes a point that culture can oppress very powerfully:

> As I look back to when I sat on my grandfather's knee, I can see grand-father teaching me about Jesus . . . The image of this blonde, blue-eyed Jesus was on every church wall, in every home, over every dining table. Visual imagery is so important, so powerful that, although I had been told that he was Jewish, for all that I knew of him, because I had no other visual image of him, these images got the better of me and he was white, and British – like me. In retrospect, thinking about draw-ing, even at school we did not draw black people, because there were no positive black images in the books that we could copy. So British meant white. I was almost into middle age before I began to see black young people who didn't have straight hair as beautiful, that comes from my childhood. I have been back home on holiday to Bedford and sitting in the pew in my old church, looking at that painting on the wall, it almost revolted me. It is still there, misleading children all over again.   (Sybil Phoenix in Hooker and Sargant, undated, p. 99)

Oppression also happens at a structural level where social, economic or political dimensions come into play. Social factors include class, gender, race and other social divisions. Political factors include the distribution of power at a formal (political structures level) and in-formal (power relations between groups and individuals). Economic factors relate to the distribution of wealth and other resources. Each of the three areas – personal, cultural, structural – are interrelated, and oppression needs to be engaged with and addressed at each level. A youth worker thinking about why a black young man is not doing well at school may engage with personal and cultural elements but probably structural too as she looks at how there are patterns of achievement among different social groups. In different denominations and faith groups there are roles that are not available to women, using the PCS analysis; that is structural oppression, although some may believe it has a theological rationale.

Theological perspectives

The Northumbria Community <www.northumbriacommunity.org> is a network of people who are seeking to explore ways of living out the Christian faith in today's culture; they are seen as part of the 'new monasticism' that is emerging in the UK and beyond. The Northumbria Community has as its rule availability and vulnerability. These concepts are both challenging and liberating in working with diversity. Paul has found that these principles give him a way of living and relating in difficult circumstances, particularly when he feels he is on shaky ground.

Acknowledging that we are vulnerable, that all of us have vulnerabilities, helps us emphasize our common humanity and realize that all of us will seem different in some particular context. Availability emphasizes a willingness for God to use us in whatever way he leads and for us to have an attitude of expectation that the Holy Spirit may prompt us to engage with people or situations that we would never have anticipated. Richard Foster (1980, p. 122) suggests praying, 'Lord Jesus, I would so appreciate it if You would bring me someone today whom I can serve.' If we have the courage to pray this that should enhance our diversity skills! This may also introduce us to 'people of peace' (Luke 10.6) who are instrumental in further developing our ministry or opening new doors. In our experience both individuals and agencies can be 'people of peace', and being open to who God brings across our path, for us to work with, may reap many benefits.

Aston Villa FC were exploring how they could expand their ground. There were already good interfaith relationships in the area and the vicar was chair of the local mosques and churches group. The Villa invited local residents to discuss the proposal. There had been a mixed relationship between the football club and the local community. One of the final proposals that the football club put forward was to build a stand where there was currently a road. This was unacceptable to local residents as this was a major road through the area and would change the feel of the area in a detrimental way, moving more traffic along already busy roads, disrupting bus routes, etc. Villa moved ahead with this plan. The local community decided they were going to object. It was planned that one Sunday they would make a human chain around the ground. Some of the community made an even stronger stand by coming to protest in their Villa shirts. At a given time the community linked arms, black to white to Asian, to make a prophetic statement to the club and the local authority in charge of planning. The outcome was that the stand was built on stilts over the road; the road remains open today because diverse people collaborated over a common enemy.

The body of Christ is for many one of the foremost theological drivers and motivators towards working diversely in collaboration. In 1 Corinthians 12, St Paul explores the metaphor of a body and how it works best when its different parts respect each other and work together: 'Gifts are shared out among Christians; all do not receive the same gift, but all gifts come from the Spirit, so that there is no room for rivalry, discontent, or a feeling of superiority' (Barrett, 1971, pp. 283–4). Although this text is about Christians there are relevant principles for wider collaborative ministry, particularly in reflecting on who has the gifts and where they are located within our communities or collaborative ministry contexts. Again, we need to be self-aware and realize our background can impact how we see others and regard ourselves and that having this corporate vision of a body may help us realize the value of being inclusive.

Sometimes our theology is shaped by something we hear. Paul was on a retreat with the late Bishop of Aston, John Austin, who challenged the newly ordained 'to remember that not only are you there for the salvation of your parishioners but they are also there for your salvation'. This became a paradigm shift for Paul's ministry as it changed the way he served others. He actively became more open to being affected by their lives and experiences and to be willing to be changed by those he served rather than seeing it as his responsibility to change those around him. This relates back to our chapter on reflecting. This is the essence of diversity in collaborative ministry, to learn, change, be refined with and by others for the sake of our Christ-likeness and more effective service in God's kingdom.

A computer is a helpful metaphor for an understanding of the place of diversity in ministry. You need a hard drive, screen, software, etc. for a computer to work. It is difficult to say what is the most important. Without a screen it doesn't matter how powerful your hard drive is or how large your memory if you cannot see what work you have done. If you have no operating system what use are programmes? None of us has much idea how a computer works, all of us get frustrated when they do not work properly but we all realize that one small part malfunctioning can stop everything else from doing what it is created to do. The role of leaders in collaborative ministry may sometimes need to be to make sure that everyone is functioning well so that the whole works. We need to appreciate that the whole works much better when the sum of the parts are not only present but connected together.

Perspectives on diversity

This section contains stories that illustrate the joys (and some of the pains) of using our diversity skills with the hope that it will provide both insights and a challenge.

Ecumenical

While Paul was working in a parish he began a collaborative project with another church, which was the fruit of both churches reflecting individually and then realizing the solution was to be found in working together. His church had run a children's second-hand clothes shop but then the shop closed and his church relied on the parent and toddler group to maintain sales. It plodded along but those involved realized it was not being as effective as it could be. Meanwhile the local Methodist church had a purpose-built charity shop at the front of their church but they were struggling with local volunteers. They had also undertaken an audit of the local community and top of the residents' request list was somewhere to meet. Collaboration between Paul and the Methodist minister resulted in 'Aston Link'; the clothes from Paul's church went to the Methodist shop and some of his volunteers went to what had become a new project owned, staffed and run by the two churches together. At the end they were offering food two lunchtimes a week, legal and housing advice through visits from a local project worker, the shop itself, trips to the seaside, family activities, Christmas Day lunch and finally a worship option. It involved a corporate vision, lay leadership, sacrificing one project, working to each other's gifts and strengths, taking risks, providing a safe place for those who needed it and a good meal twice a week, and a profit to use to subsidize the trips and other activities. We learnt and reflected together that corporate resurrection can follow individual death. Why do separately what we can do better together? This fulfils the biblical mandate to show God's love through the way we work together, prefer each other's needs and see good in each other.

The local Churches Together group worked very well. They met regularly for prayer and a 24-hour annual retreat; there were corporate mission ventures together as well as regular schools work. Sometimes it was hard to balance everyone's agenda but the effort was felt to be worth it to reflect the commitment and respect the ministers and churches had towards each other. This was a good model as it was also honest in those things where agreement was not possible, which was predominantly around baptism. Several of the denominations felt that they could not accept the infant baptism practice of others. These church leaders said if a member changed churches and 'only' had infant baptism, they would encourage the individual to be baptized again. This was not appreciated by some of the ministers, but others were not for moving. It was a true and honest example of agreeing to disagree for the greater good of unity and the furtherance of the kingdom of God.

Multi-faith collaboration

One of the contemporary challenges for collaborative ministry is multi-faith collaboration. Paul is Senior Chaplain in the NHS in Birmingham; there multi-faith collaborative ministry is a given. However, some of his past colleagues express surprise that he can do that job as a professed evangelical. For him it is about having a common agenda, shared commitments, a belief in equality of opportunity and a passion to see people receiving appropriate religious, spiritual and pastoral care so that as individuals they are treated appropriately, with dignity and in their best interest. When in a parish it was about seeing a community regenerated and faiths working together to this end.

There are two particular issues we want to highlight around multi-faith collaborative ministry and these are gender and prayer. Paul has forgotten how many times he has inappropriately offered his hand to a Muslim woman (which culturally would not be the usual practice); usually they have been gracious enough to accept. But he has learnt to act in ways that avoid their being in an awkward position. Asking honest questions may be better than making assumptions as with all faiths there are different streams which may have a variety of practices. When Paul leads staff meetings they have a reflection time at the beginning. He chooses not to pray, so that people in the team do not feel compromised or assume that he thinks we all believe in the same God. An area that needs special attention is the use of sensitive and inclusive language and an understanding that words are heard differently depending on culture, gender, age and so on.

The NHS has a mandate to provide religious, pastoral and spiritual care and there are five values or ethical principles that underpin this and these may provide insights into our collaborative ministry. One is equality and an emphasis in believing in the equal worth of everyone; no one is of more or less value than someone else. Another is that you work in the best interest of a person; this could be a valuable insight for collaborative ministry teams. Treating people with dignity is a principle but we have to know about them to know what that means in their context. The final two are responsibility and rights; we have sometimes put the emphasis on one rather than the other, in ministry often the former and in the community perhaps the latter.

Interdisciplinary work

At Birmingham Children's Hospital there is a Clinical Ethics Advisory Group. Anyone, including patients or their parents, can refer an ethical dilemma to the group. For example, who should get the transplant if a liver becomes available, the very sick child who needs a temporary liver until they can get a joint liver and small bowel or the less sick child who only needs a liver? The group works well because there are so many perspectives, e.g. nurses, doctors, lawyers, a professional ethicist, chaplain, physiotherapist and so on. There is considerable diversity within the group's 20 or so members and in a recent case the group changed its response after a late contribution from a specific perspective. As you can imagine, with so many intelligent, articulate minds brought to bear from different perspectives on one issue it is never a dull affair! The group's strong capacity to offer helpful advice lies in its diverse make-up and its members sharpening each other as they debate and seek a common mind.

Personality

At the Midlands Centre for Youth Ministry we introduce students to the Myers-Briggs Type Indicator™. We constantly emphasize that we are all different and that valuing these differences is fundamental to effective working together. A couple of the books we draw on give a flavour of what it sometimes feels like in collaborative work: *I'm Not Crazy, I'm Just Not You* (Pearman, 1998) and *Was That Really Me? How Everyday Stress Brings out Our Hidden Personality* (Quenk, 2002). Paul and Sally are complete opposites in Myers-Briggs preferences and have had to learn to value each other's way of working but also when to compromise and find a shared solution that works for both of them. For example, Sally likes things planned well in advance and would describe herself as well organized. Paul gets energized as a deadline approaches and does his best work then. Understanding such things in a collaborative ministry team helps to recognize some of the frustrations but may also lead to some ground rules or boundaries around how work needs to be done so everyone feels that they can flourish.

Personality

As we reflect on diversity in collaborative ministry, the area of personality and gifting comes to mind quickly. It can be good to take the opportunity to be honest as to why some of us do not do collaborative ministry well. Some of us can be quite independent in nature and prefer to work on our own, others believe that no one will do a job as well as us so prefer to do it ourselves. Another reason is insecurity in the light of those who are around us. We can easily perceive others to be more gifted than we are or feel that they are more appreciated. Sometimes the shadow of those in our past or present causes us to think less of ourselves and this impacts the way that we try to do collaborative ministry. The impact of this can be the fight-or-flight responses that we discussed in Chapter 8 on defence mechanisms. Being aware of our vulnerabilities in this area or even talking them through with someone we trust may be beneficial in trying to overcome the barriers such thoughts may throw up.

Cultural

In many ministry contexts there is a diversity of cultural backgrounds and it can sometimes feel like crossing a bit of a minefield to navigate them. Della was aware that some of the church thought she was a bit posh as she had a professional job, unlike most of the other women in the congregation. In a professional context she would challenge sexist language or express a preference not to be called 'Love' or something similar but felt that if she did that in the church context it would be experienced as oppressive and accentuate differences. Also, the church favoured a kiss on the cheek during the 'peace' in the Communion service, and she felt she needed to join in so she didn't seem racist or a snob despite a preference for a simple handshake. In Christianity it sometimes feels as if we are expected to conform to a class culture rather than a Christian or biblical one, and we may benefit from some honest conversation about how our culture may be experienced by those who are new or who are in some way different from the majority.

Decision-making

One role Paul and Sally had in Youth for Christ was to manage year-out teams. The policy in selecting individuals to join a project was that everyone on the interview team, which would include new and experienced staff as well as one of the current volunteers, had to be part of a unanimous decision. The objective of having consensus on everyone we took was sometimes a difficult process but Paul and Sally were committed in encouraging all voices to be heard. The outcome of this policy was that no member of staff could say in later months they did not want to support any individual because they did not think they should be on the programme. Working out how you are going to take decisions in collaborative ministry is an important step but certainly ample time should be given so that voices can be heard and the possibility of achieving consensus is maximized.

Challenges and issues

There are many challenges and issues that come with working with people and agencies who are not Christians. In a multi-faith context, how do we deal with prayer? Does each faith group offer a prayer from their own tradition? Do we have a period of silence or ignore the whole area? When in a multicultural parish, Paul and Sally invited neighbours to social events but in doing so needed to ensure that there was either vegetarian food or a halal meat alternative. When invited to a neighbour's house they had to come to terms with the fact that the wife did not join in but remained in the kitchen cooking the meal. Challenging the practice of someone in their own home seems both ungracious and disrespectful.

Working collaboratively with local faith groups in community regeneration, or working together against Aston Villa's proposed development, didn't stop local churches in Aston from knocking on doors with a *Jesus* video in a variety of languages. There was a desire to maintain the Christian identity and mission and to remain faithful to what was seen as God's calling to be salt and light. Steve Chalke describes it as the difference between a fruit salad and a fruit puree: keeping the distinct flavours and textures of a fruit salad is possible within collaborative ministry, it doesn't have to be a nondescript mush! There are also tensions because of the diversity of practices and beliefs among Christians and a need to acknowledge that some Christians behave in ways that others feel are inappropriate and the confusion that this can cause when trying to work together.

An important issue to acknowledge and raise is that all human beings have prejudices and that we need to have a redemptive attitude towards our heart and spirit and be honest about our feelings. Most of us will fight a tendency to think less of people who are different from us whether that be issues of appearance, personality, sexuality, gender, age, ethnicity or disability. Some of us will also have a tendency to start a statement with 'Some of my best friends are Black/gay/Sikhs/socialists/Anglicans/Manchester United supporters', before going on to make an offensive or oppressive statement. Conversation, education and dialogue are ways of meeting this challenge. It is much harder to be prejudiced against people when we have got to know them and have begun to understand some of the issues from their perspective. We need to be honest too about the way that we can be influenced by the media and the way different groups are portrayed. We can only move forward if we face our fears and prejudices honestly and uncover the wrong attitudes we may have uncritically adopted.

Paul admits a need to be honest and say that his early journey has had a profound effect on his current values and perspectives. As he reflected on his attitude while living in the inner city and relating to those of different faiths, it never occurred to him in those early days that he had anything to learn from anyone who was not a Christian. His logic was, How can I have anything to learn from someone who does not have Jesus as their way, truth and the life? Looking back, he is ashamed of his ignorance. Sometimes we talk about tolerating differences but is that really enough? How would you feel if someone walked up to you and said, 'I tolerate you'? Probably not very encouraged. We must make a journey beyond tolerance to respect and hopefully appreciation too.

A final issue to discuss is whether or not we place any boundaries around who we will or will not work with. This is a decision that perhaps needs to be thought through in advance of an opportunity. A classic in some church and Christian communities has been around accepting funding from the lottery. There are passionate beliefs on both sides of the argument but such decisions need to be informed and articulated clearly so everyone understands the rationale.

If you find yourself working in a diverse collaborative context then many of the exercises and ideas in previous chapters may well be useful in helping you to understand each other better and move towards working together effectively.

Growing in diversity skills

This is some of the advice we have for growing in diversity skills.

- Be courageous, take risks, have tenacity, perseverance and patience.
- Aim to see the good in each other and have an attitude of equal but different; encourage many voices.
- Discern priorities. What can we agree to disagree on? What are the non-negotiables? Celebrate more than mourn diversity.
- Audit our attitudes and our work; face our fears and insecurities.
- Appreciate the benefit of diverse corporate wisdom.
- Imitate and demonstrate the image and nature of our Trinitarian God; in building community fulfil the mandate of body ministry.
- Be secure enough to encourage others and listen to them even when you know what they say will be different from what you believe or value.

Points for reflection, discussion and action

- Do you genuinely value diversity?
- What sort of differences are most problematic to you?

- Are you aware of what your prejudices are? How do you confront them?
- What are the challenges that you face in developing collaborative ministry beyond your usual partners?

10

Evaluation skills

Socrates says, 'An unexamined life is not worth living.' Those who are passionate about evaluation may want to adapt this to say, 'An unevaluated project is not worth running.' We need to acknowledge that evaluation goes on whether or not we formalize it; we all make judgements and assessments of ministry we experience or participate in. Think about what happens over Sunday lunch after a church service in some households! However, just because informal evaluation occurs is not a good reason to avoid a formalized approach at appropriate times. We do need to realize too that evaluation can sometimes be scary or threatening as many of us find it hard to think about being judged, which is how evaluation is sometimes presented or experienced.

Here is an example of the starting point for a piece of evaluation by Dave Wiles, Chief Executive of Frontier Youth Trust. His reflections will help him and the organization concerned do things differently another time. So often we avoid asking these hard questions:

> Three young people I worked with became Christians, I was thrilled and as I carved another notch in my Bible I bathed in the knowledge of heavenly parties! The trouble started a few years later when I realized that one of the young people was in prison (again!) and that the other had come to see me to check how he could undo his decision to be a Christian as it was too demanding. The third still lives near to me and we see each other regularly – he's stuck with it. Well, perhaps a 33 per cent 'success' rate is not too bad! Or is it? What went wrong?

What is evaluation?

Evaluation at its simplest involves asking some questions, answering those questions, analysing, reflecting and assessing the evidence and then implementing what we have learnt through the process. More formally,

Evaluation is assessing and judging the value of a piece of work, an organisation or a service. Its main purpose is to help an organisation reflect on what it is trying to achieve, assessing how far it is succeeding, and identify required changes. (Del Tufo, 2002)

Subhra (2004, p. 15) offers these elements as comprising the purpose of evaluation:

- provides accountability to all stakeholders, not just funders;
- should be an educational and learning process, from which communities, workers and funders all benefit;
- builds credibility with funders;
- helps a project see where it is going and if the direction needs to be changed;
- shares experiences;
- celebrates achievements;
- reflects on the strengths of the group;
- improves the quality and planning of future work;
- determines whether the effort was effective and worthwhile.

Evaluation is often a delicate balance between service improvement and proving the value of a service to funders or stakeholders. Evaluation can make a positive difference:

- A regional organization identified a new piece of work to do and raised £50,000 of external funding for it.
- A community project worked hard on evaluating the first grant they received and then unexpectedly received a second one because of the quality of the data from the first evaluation.
- A children's project invited an external evaluator in who uncovered some difficult team dynamics; once these had been identified formally the management committee had to deal with the issue rather than dismissing it.
- A church had an outreach project that had lost its way and there was little commitment to or interest in it. An evaluation identified some different needs and the project was reframed to respond to the current community context rather than the one that existed when it was established 20 years ago.

There are different approaches to evaluation and which one we choose will partly determine how we undertake the process and what is found out. There are at least six different approaches (Worthen *et al.*, cited in O'Sullivan, 2004, p. 7):

- *Objectives* Focuses on objectives to determine to what extent they have been achieved.
- *Management* Focuses on finding out information to assist decision-makers.
- *Consumer* Looks at projects and programmes to determine their relative worth.
- *Expertise* Establishes peer and professional judgements of quality.
- *Adversary* Examines projects and programmes from pro and con perspectives.
- *Participant* Addresses stakeholders' needs for information.

We may need a mix of these different approaches to undertake a thorough evaluation. Collaborative ministry warrants a commitment to consultation and participation which is shared between stakeholders, leaders and those doing the evaluation.

Evaluation can be undertaken by someone or a team internal to the organization, by peers from another organization where perhaps you set up a reciprocal arrangement, or by an appropriate external person. Which approach you take may well be driven by resources available and the scope of the evaluation proposed. Evaluation isn't done in isolation; we need to bear in mind those doing and managing the work, the clients or service users of the work, and those whom the work impacts, such as the community, and wider policy issues. Ensure that whoever is undertaking the evaluation can relate well to all the different people who will need to be consulted. This is particularly important for service users with specific needs.

Theological perspectives

While some will see evaluation as a secular management tool, there are clear biblical examples that we can draw on to see the benefits for us of including evaluation as part of what we do to be effective in collaborative ministry. Genesis tells us that God made an assessment on what he had done and saw that it was good (1.31); reading Leviticus, Numbers and Deuteronomy can be interpreted as setting rules and standards to work to; God encourages recording events to report and retell (Nehemiah and Jeremiah); resource allocation is seen in the story of Gideon (Judges 7); needs analysis and the setting of outcomes can be seen in the stories of the rich young ruler (Mark 10.17–30), the Great Commission (Matthew 28.19) and the parable of the sheep and the goats (Matthew 25.31–46); Paul often seems to be advocating a see, act, review approach in his letters and uses metaphors that imply measurement and achievement – builders (1 Corinthians 3.12–16), athletes (2 Timothy 2.5), soldiers (Ephesians 6.10–13); the analysis of churches in Revelation 2 and 3 also suggests an evaluative approach (based on ideas from Nigel Pimlott). Hudson argues that:

> Evaluation is one of God's ways of bringing the history of the past into dialogue with the hope for the future . . . We are called into new growth and new ministries by taking a realistic and hopeful look at what we have been and what we can still become.   (1998, p. 7)

Evaluation brief

Before we begin an evaluation it is important to have thought through a range of issues and ideally to have a brief so all are clear on what is happening, why, where, how and when (see <www.ces-vol.org> for more guidance). If the evaluation is being undertaken by anyone outside of the organization then this is vital. It can be useful to begin by gathering all the written information that is available that provides a helpful background to the rest of the evaluation such as monitoring data, annual reports, etc. Questions to be covered by the brief include:

- What is the purpose of the evaluation?
- What do we want to find out?
- What are the key questions to be asked?
- What are the indicators we are measuring? These can include such things as access, availability, relevance, development, change, quality, efficiency, impact, participation, involvement, results.
- Who is to be consulted?
- What methods may be most appropriate?
- Is it all or only part of the organization that is being evaluated?
- How will the evaluation be used?
- Who will see the report and how will it be disseminated?
- What about issues around confidentiality and access to service users?

- What work will be done and by whom?
- What are the time frame and budget?

We recommend discussing the answers to these questions together so that the evaluation is owned and understood by all who will be impacted by it. In thinking about what elements of the organization we are evaluating here are some ideas to prompt thinking:

- time, priorities, organization, planning . . .
- communication, reports . . .
- supervision, accountability, support . . .
- policies, procedures, good practice . . .
- teamwork, delegation, decision-making . . .
- administration, paperwork . . .
- ability to manage stress, conflict, change . . .
- finance, IT, equipment . . .
- record-keeping, monitoring, evaluation . . .
- vision, goals, aims, objectives . . .
- training, development, learning . . .
- motivation, timekeeping, reliability, integrity . . . .

Ethics

There are several ethical issues involved in carrying out evaluation. Evaluation is always going to be value-laden and we bring assumptions to the process which will impact what is evaluated, the questions asked, methods used, data collected and the interpretation and presentation of findings. For example, evaluations can have both a covert and an overt purpose. If there are possible consequences of an evaluation that may have a serious impact on people, such as the closure of a project, it may be important to ensure that agendas are clear and the range of possibilities articulated (sensitively) beforehand. It is important to be aware of personal bias and the dangers of constructing an evaluation to prove a point or to comply with others' expectations, particularly funders.

Another issue is a tendency to sometimes carry out an evaluation because you have to but then not follow through on the recommendations. This can build up a culture of cynicism if evaluation takes place but nothing ever changes. Ethical presentation of data is important; for example, there is a difference between the number of young people contacted by an agency and the number of contacts that an agency has with young people. 'Is this ethical?' is a question to ask before you implement your evaluation process.

Personal evaluation

A survey of over 200 youth workers (Pimlott, 2008, p. 17) found that although there was a commitment from many to evaluation it seemed to be more focused on the young people they worked with rather than on improving their own practice. As well as evaluating the project or work we are involved in we may want to encourage members of the collaborative ministry team to undertake a personal evaluation. This list of questions for individuals (developed from Pyle and Seals, 1995, pp. 134–7) is generic and they can be adapted or supplemented depending on the context:

- How do you see and value yourself? Are you able to take good care of yourself? Do you seek praise or deflect compliments?
- Do you live a life of personal integrity and consistency?
- Are you self-aware and realize your impact on others? Do you know how your past impacts the present? Can you own both your strengths and weaknesses?
- Have you got an active devotional life and a growing relationship with God?
- Are you dependable and trustworthy, and do you keep confidences?
- Can you build honest and open relationships? Do you value the diversity and worth of people?
- Can you exercise appropriate discipline or self-control including the ability to take personal responsibility and initiative where appropriate?
- Are you able to respond well to constructive feedback? Can you give feedback to others?
- Do you listen well and attentively with ears, eyes and heart?
- Can you make good decisions taking into account the relevant information without being too hasty or prevaricating too much?
- How do you respond to stress? How does stress manifest in your behaviour? Have you identified appropriate coping mechanisms?

- What is your response to conflict? Do you avoid or enjoy? Have you developed ways of engaging constructively with conflict?
- Do you work well collaboratively? What roles do you tend to undertake?
- How do you respond to those in authority? Does who is leading you impact the way you respond to them?
- What sort of leader are you? Can you draw on a variety of leadership styles?
- Can you organize, prioritize and delegate work? Can you equip others to do their work and accept they may do it differently from you?
- Do you communicate effectively verbally and in writing in a range of contexts to different groups of people?

In teaching a module on leadership and strategy Sally started with an exercise where students were encouraged to evaluate their leadership skills against a range of models of leadership and to use these to evaluate themselves as a leader as the course progressed. Often it is hard to change a project without seeing changes in the people who work on it and a holistic evaluation may involve individuals evaluating themselves as well as the work the project does.

Methods and tools for evaluation

Evaluation can be quantitative, qualitative or both. Quantitative evaluation is about counting and measuring numbers and qualitative is concerned with observing and listening to feelings, processes, experiences, events, meanings and understandings. Formative evaluation may happen on a regular basis and involves identifying changes that have taken place, making judgements as to the quality of the work and noting learning and development that has taken place. Summative evaluation would usually happen at the end of the project or programme and seeks to show to what extent the objectives have been achieved.

There are a range of tools outlined below which can be used in evaluation. It is best practice to get informed consent when we do any sort of research, and evaluation can be classified as research. This involves making clear what we are doing, on whose behalf, what will happen to the results, that participation is voluntary and that individuals can withdraw while this is practical, i.e. before the final report is written up. It may also be that there are ideas in Chapter 5 on Vision-building that can be adapted for evaluation. There are also more complex approaches to evaluation which can be found in the literature (see Shaw *et al.*, 2006, for example), which some may be familiar with from their professional backgrounds and may want to adapt for the ministry context. There is not space to do justice to the range of such approaches here.

Storytelling

There are several reasons why using stories is beneficial in evaluation (see Rixon, 2006). The first is that stories are an engaging medium for participants. Stories provide insight as things emerge that are perhaps not expected, and help with sense-making in the organization; they also reveal the organizational memory. Perhaps one of the most helpful attributes of stories is that they can be used to explore difficult issues; they can convey messages that are otherwise hard to hear.

In helping people to tell their story, one of the key things is to craft the questions properly which means helping them to remember. It can be better to use words such as experiences or events rather than story as sometimes we think that story is fiction and thus are not sure what that means when we talk about things that have happened. One of the ways of doing this is to ask questions that try to elicit feelings as this often evokes memories. A simple way in is to ask: 'When have you felt . . .' and add in the most appropriate word depending on what you are trying to evaluate, for example, most proud, appreciated, disappointed, encouraged, fulfilled (Callahan *et al.*, 2006). Sometimes adding several options of emotions can be helpful as a word triggers a memory. We suggest introducing our question with a phrase like imagine, think about, reflect on, consider and give the broader context of the question. This sort of approach can be used with a group to try and draw out elements of the corporate story.

In adopting a more straightforwardly narrative approach to the storytelling we can ask a range of people to prepare their stories to present individually to the rest of the group (see Evaluation Trust Toolkit for fuller details). When they have told their stories we can explore questions in four key areas: What? (description) Why? (explanation) So what? (synthesis) Now what? (action). We may spend around an hour per story on this activity.

Having introduced the process, the storyteller is invited to tell their story to the evaluation brief given. This should be done without interruption. At the end people are given a few minutes to note their reflections on the story in relation to the bigger picture, and to think about how far their own experience is similar to or different from the story they have heard. At this stage questions are asked, with someone assigned responsibility to note what comes out of the exercise. For example:

- What were the problems/issues/needs? What did you do? What were the successes/difficulties?
- Why do you think it happened? Why did you/they react as you/they did? Why did you do what you did (the strategies or actions)? Why do you think it worked/didn't work?
- What have we learned? What remains confusing? How did people or relationships change? What unexpected outcomes occurred?
- What will we do differently next time? What will be our next set of actions? What are the key lessons?

It is important to then reflect on all the discussions and summarize what has been learnt and needs to be taken forward and what actions need to be proposed or taken.

Numerical measurement

Numbers can be collected on many things, e.g. how many people are using a service, income and expenditure, hours of provision or work, accessibility and diversity, the range of activities. Most evaluations will include some quantitative data which hopefully can be accessed through existing records, etc.

Reviewing documents and records

Some evaluation can take place by going through the records and paperwork that already exists and seeing how this information answers the questions being asked. This is helpfully done by someone who is familiar with the material as they understand how it has been compiled and what it means.

Observation

Observation can make a significant contribution to an evaluation as it can draw out data that may not be available through any other method. It is a skilled task and needs to be undertaken once we have clearly identified what it is we are trying to find out. It can be useful in seeing if what is done is consistent with what the agency said is done. It can be beneficial in a ministry context where relationships are so important and there can sometimes be a reluctance to disclose some of the problems and issues that the team are facing. Observation can be done by a participant or an external observer but it needs to be noted that if people know that they are being observed they may well change their behaviour because of it.

If undertaking an observation it can be beneficial to draw a diagram that maps the area and where people and objects are. In a room, 'objects' means furniture, etc.; in an open space 'objects' refers to such things as seats or shops. For example, you may evaluate your youth club by seeing who uses what. Who is on the computers? Who plays pool? Who talks to the leaders? Who is on the seat outside smoking? This is partly to assess the effectiveness of what you are providing but also to look at issues such as gender, peer groups, age groups, and see whether there are patterns that may help you develop what you do. You may do an observation after a service at church to assess how welcoming or inclusive your church is to newcomers or across generations. We can do an observation where we note everything that happens in a specific time period or observe what happens in a particular place or sample every five minutes, for example. Look out for power dynamics, who is included, excluded, responses, body language, interactions. We need to work out a clear way of recording our data and analysing it.

Questionnaires and surveys

This involves asking several people the same set of questions and then analysing the results. If doing a questionnaire always pilot it to ensure that it is understood, that we are finding out what we thought we would and that it is accessible for the target group. For example, what would a seven-year-old do with a box that says 'for the sick'? Not always put money in it!

Write questions as concisely and clearly as possible. Begin with the simplest questions and leave anything sensitive or more complex towards the end. Think carefully about all the data being gathered and don't ask about things like age or income unless they are vital to the evaluation. Think about how to analyse the data when you formulate the questions. Use tick boxes or other easy-to-summarize approaches but make sure a good range of responses has been identified or have an 'other' category where an answer can be specified. Rating on a scale of 1–6 or 1–10, or the equivalent in words, can be helpful (avoid an odd number as there can be a temptation to choose the middle number). Use open questions where necessary and make sure there is space for them to be completed.

Don't ask leading questions or make assumptions in the way questions are asked. It can be beneficial to add 'Don't know' as a category to avoid people having to choose an answer they may not agree with. Make sure instructions are clear and people know where to return the questionnaire to. Making questionnaires anonymous can help with honesty of answers. Have a final open-ended question, which gives participants the opportunity to add anything else they would like to. Try to avoid going over more than two sides of paper and do not use a font size smaller than 11 points.

Interviewing

Although interviews can be time-consuming they are an effective way of learning in depth what someone thinks of a project or piece of work. Interviews can be unstructured, semi-structured or structured.

Unstructured interviews mean you ask whatever questions occur to you as you go along. These can be less helpful with evaluation as there is often no consistency between interviews, data can be hard to analyse and in retrospect we can realize that we have not found out what we needed.

Structured interviews are the sort of thing that market researchers do, where each person is asked the same question in the same way and this can feel a little restrictive in evaluation.

The best option perhaps is a semi-structured interview where you have a list of questions but with the flexibility to change the order and ask supplementary questions depending on how the interview goes.

As with questionnaires, pilot your questions, ensure the wording is clear and not open to misinterpretation. When setting up the interview think through issues of informed consent, confidentiality and recording. You may do interviews face to face or over the telephone or even through instant messaging. Think through the benefits and drawbacks of each for your context and the individuals you are going to contact and what may suit them best. Try and put the person at ease, demonstrate good listening skills (see Chapter 7 on supervision) and thank them for their participation. With interviews think how long each will take, how you will transcribe them if recorded and how you will analyse the data. Try to keep interviews to an hour at the maximum.

Focus groups

Focus groups involve getting a small group of people (usually between six and 12) together with a facilitator who guides them through a few relevant questions or topics and ensures that the discussion continues to be relevant. In a focus group there is an element of constructing a shared understanding or meaning and people interact, change and develop their ideas. A group would usually last between 30 and 90 minutes depending on the participants. To gain the most from the data we would usually record (with permission) the group or have someone else make detailed notes of what happens. An important part of a focus group is getting a comfortable and safe environment where people feel free to talk. Beginning with refreshments can help relax people. Make sure ground rules are agreed before starting and that people know how what is said will be used and what the purpose of it is. Emphasize confidentiality and don't forget to thank people for their participation. Usually the facilitator will say little apart from asking questions and steering the conversation to ensure that the necessary data is collected. Facilitators should not participate in the conversation and should remain neutral but demonstrate good active listening skills. Chapter 3 on facilitation elaborates on these points.

The head, heart, carrier bag and dustbin exercise

Take a large piece of paper with a body drawn on it with a head and a big heart along with a carrier bag and a dustbin. Give each participant four post-it notes and ask them to write something in each of these categories:

1 one post-it for the head – something I've learnt from being part of this project . . . ;
2 one post-it for the heart – something I've felt/experienced from being part of this project . . . ;

3 one post-it for the carrier bag – something I'll take away from being part of this project . . . ;

4 one post-it for the dustbin – anything I want to forget or that was not so good about being part of this project . . . .

Then stick all the notes on to the relevant part of the poster and either discuss it with the group who are there, or take it away and analyse the findings for yourself and others involved in the event, and summarize the learning for a future event. Remember you may want to keep examples of what people actually say for future publicity or reporting back to stakeholders. (This version from Evaluation Trust Toolkit.)

Visual tools

One useful tool is the Blob picture (see <www.pipwilson.com>), which comes in a variety of incarnations and we can ask people where they see themselves in the picture and why. Perhaps the most famous of these is the Blob tree where blobby-shaped people are engaged in various activities, e.g. sitting on a branch at the end far from anyone, or on a tree swing, or sawing off a branch, or beginning to climb up. Individuals are encouraged to look at the picture and say which blob they most identify with and why, or even draw themselves in the picture. We can ask people to take photographs reflecting specific aspects of the work or we can create collages or pictures in response to specific questions.

Presenting findings

The material gained during the evaluation process needs to be analysed, interpreted, synthesized, summarized and presented in an appropriate format for our context. This is a simple guide to the process. Begin by organizing the data you have collected, categorizing it where possible and start to identify emerging themes. Colour pens and/or codes can be useful in this process.

The analysis can be facilitated by asking questions such as:

- What are the similarities? Differences?
- What stands out? What is unexpected or unusual?
- Are there patterns? Common themes?

Interpreting the data is the next stage, answering questions such as:

- Are we accomplishing our aims? Meeting our objectives?
- Which findings have particular significance?
- What are the outcomes of what we do? How and why is our work (in)effective?
- What have we learned through evaluation?
- What do we need to do about it?

Finally you need to consider what needs to be communicated, to whom and what is the most effective method of doing this. Think about the range of stakeholders and also how your evaluation may impact the bigger picture of policy development.

Reports usually follow a similar format which is as follows:

- title and contents page
- executive summary
- introduction which sets the context of the organization and evaluation
- evaluation process, including purpose, focus and methodology
- findings
- conclusions and recommendations
- appendices, including any bibliography, people consulted (not service users), any questionnaires, etc. used.

There are a variety of things we can do with our evaluation apart from producing a traditional paper report. Posters, CDs or websites may all be more accessible ways of sharing the information. We can also decide if the information can be summarized in a more ongoing user-friendly format such as a list of practice principles, dos and don'ts, manifesto, guidebook, etc. Where we have permission and can ensure anonymity then using case studies and personal histories can communicate what we do more powerfully than more formal categories. If we have the relevant expertise we may wish to disseminate our findings through an academic journal article. Having a meeting to share and discuss the findings might be helpful, particularly if a range of possible changes have emerged. Evaluation results can also be useful in promotion and marketing if they demonstrate something we would like to be known more widely. It may be also that they demonstrate a gap or potential development area that we may wish to raise funds for, or partner another agency in. We may also want to use our evaluation to produce a press release or as the basis of an interview with local radio or television.

Points for reflection, discussion and action

- How do you feel about evaluation? Are your previous experiences positive, negative or neutral?
- What are your current evaluation practices? Are they focused more on learning or proving?
- Which approach to evaluation is most appropriate to your context?
- What needs evaluating? When? Who should be involved?
- Have you made the best use of the material gained from evaluation?

11

Conclusion

Collaborative ministry may not always be the easiest context to work in but it can be creative, inspiring, challenging and an example of the kingdom at work. In this book we have explored a range of skills that enhance such ministry and at this stage we recommend identifying which your team would benefit from working on. In the belief that it is good if different parts of the body play to their strengths, it may be helpful to allocate different areas among the team and have one person champion each area and perhaps take responsibility for auditing and facilitating training in that skill.

Do the right things but do them right

A crucial insight for collaborative ministry is Drucker's differentiation between doing things right or doing the right things (cited in Thompson, 2006, p. 55). In collaborative ministry it can be that we are doing the right things but we are not doing things right in terms of people or processes and that causes many of the problems. The skills discussed in this book have been chosen in the hope that they will help teams to do things right as well as to do the right things.

This is a comment about doing things right from one of our students who was involved in a piece of collaborative youth work. He observes that:

> Churches cannot be parochial in their purposes for entering into a piece of collaborative work, there needs to be an understanding that the purpose of the work is collaborative and for the benefit of the young people . . . Instead of asking the question what will our church get out of this venture? A church needs to ask what can we give to this venture? Collaborative work in its nature needs to be sacrificial.
>
> (McDonald, 2007, p. 14)

Collaborative ministry is not something to be entered into lightly but is something that we imagine will increasingly be part of the Church's mission.

A formula which we have found helpful when thinking about our experiences of collaborative ministry is Thompson's CIA model (2006, p. 45). He exhorts us to:

- Control what we can control.
- Influence what we can influence.
- Accept those things that we can neither control nor influence.

Many of the tensions in collaborative ministry arise because we don't take this advice. It may be helpful to use this as a framework to have a discussion about how the team is functioning to help people be realistic about how it works. Sally recalls how when starting off in ministry she had the naïve idea that because she would be working with Christians it would be wonderful, supportive and caring! At times it might have been, but we are all flawed human beings and act in ways that are not Christ-like. Being involved in collaborative ministry changes us, hopefully for the better. We need to take responsibility for our responses and reactions to each other and look to how we can play our part in making collaborative ministry work.

Final thoughts

As we reach the end of our journey through skills for collaborative ministry we want to offer some final thoughts for those wishing to establish, maintain or develop such ministry in their setting. We have tried to distil the essence of each chapter as a prompt and reminder and perhaps a starting point for a discussion or review of your current ministry.

Collaborative ministry is a biblical model and mandate: 'He'll show us the way he works so we can live the way we're made' (Isaiah 2.3). One of the most powerful things we have to offer those outside of the Church is a flourishing community of people who respect and value each other and work together towards a common vision. True collaborative ministry is difficult to do but can be life- and community-transforming.

When involved in collaborative ministry we need to understand *group processes*. It is unrealistic to expect that groups or teams will function well together automatically. Paying attention to process is something that in our experience often gets overlooked in churches. Naming what is happening and developing strategies to move on to the performing level, or return to it after a glitch, merits serious effort as a thriving group will be infectious, others will want to join and we will accomplish more than when our energy is taken up dealing with frustration and dysfunction.

Facilitation is key to good collaborative ministry, particularly in the early stages. Think carefully about who facilitates the first meeting with a new group, and always consider co-facilitation because it models the values of collaboration. Also work hard on culture-setting right from the beginning as this will enhance the possibility of fruitful ministry.

Ministry isn't predictable and in trying to avoid a 'Groundhog day' scenario, where we keep making the same mistake time and time again, then giving time to *reflecting* on what has happened, how it happened, why it happened like that, how it might be different next time is essential. Both individual and corporate reflection is vital in keeping our collaborative ministry sharp and effective. Theological reflection provides the opportunity to integrate our faith into our reflection and emerge with an outcome that is holistic.

Vision is best created rather than caught in collaborative ministry. Working together to build vision gives a greater sense of ownership and belonging. Developing a strategy and revisiting the vision regularly is necessary to keep it as the focus of activities as it is not difficult to slide into maintenance mode from mission mode almost without realizing it.

Time given to *team-building*, if planned wisely and the rationale explained, is seldom wasted. Good relationships within a team facilitate it functioning effectively and engender a willingness to work through problems that arise rather than giving up. How the team is led will often set the tone for how it works, and helping people to identify their roles, strengths and gifts and flourish in them is part of the responsibility of leadership.

Supervision is integral to looking after people properly and ensuring that their well-being and personal and professional development are being given attention. Because of bad experiences or confusion about what is involved, often baggage comes with the idea of supervision so, as part of introducing a supervision strategy, it may be helpful to facilitate some discussion to help allay fears and build commitment for it.

Collaborative ministry without any *conflict* is probably a miracle! Try not to avoid conflict but to treat is as the normal fact of life that it is. Dealing with conflict is healthy and is something that would benefit many of us; within a church or organization it helps affirm that it is OK to express opinions (in a constructive way) and emphasizes that together we can find a way forward.

Trends in the Church and the voluntary sector suggest that we are increasingly going to need *diversity* skills because we will be working with individuals and groups who are different from us. Having the right attitude is key to working in this context; acknowledging our vulnerability and our openness to work with others is a good starting point. Being willing to take risks, not fearing for our reputation, and following where God is leading is an exciting and challenging journey.

Evaluation is about seeing in what ways our collaborative ministry is being effective and identifying ways we may develop or improve it. Evaluation should be part of our strategy and should occur on a regular basis. Having the occasional external evaluation can be encouraging but also enlightening as sometimes more emerges when the task is being taken seriously and there is perhaps more honesty when asked questions by someone who doesn't have a vested interest in the answer.

Our final question for reflection is: What is our next step in collaborative ministry? As we finished our editing residential we were fired up with lots of new ideas for writing together. The process has been creative and life-giving; we hope it will be the same for you.

Bibliography

Adair, J., *Effective Leadership: A Self-Development Model.* Aldershot, Gower, 1983.

Adair, J., *Effective Teambuilding.* London, Gower, 1986.

Adair, J., *Leadership Skills.* London, Institute of Personnel Development, 1997.

Adirondack, S., *Just About Managing? Effective Management for Voluntary Organizations and Community Groups,* 3rd edition. London, London Voluntary Service Council, 1996.

Barnes, P., *Leadership with Young People.* Lyme Regis, Russell House, 2002.

Barrett, C. K., *The First Epistle to the Corinthians,* 2nd edition. London, A. and C. Black, 1971.

Belbin, R. M., *Management Teams: Why They Succeed or Fail.* Oxford, Butterworth–Heinemann, 1981.

Belbin, R. M., *Team Roles at Work.* Oxford, Butterworth–Heinemann, 1993.

Berger, P. L., *An Invitation to Sociology.* Harmondsworth, Penguin 1972.

Berger, P. L. and Luckmann, T., *The Social Construction of Reality: A Treatise in the Sociology of Knowledge.* Garden City, New York, Anchor Books, 1966.

Bion, W. R., *Experiences in Groups and Other Papers.* London, Routledge/ Tavistock Publications, 1961.

Board of Mission, *A Time for Sharing Collaborative Ministry in Mission.* London, Board of Mission of the General Synod of the Church of England, 1995.

Brierley, D., *Joined Up.* Carlisle, Authentic, 2003.

Brierley, P., *Vision Building.* London, Hodder & Stoughton, 1989.

Brockbank, A. and McGill, I., *Facilitating Reflective Learning in Higher Education.* Buckingham, Open University Press, 1998.

Brookfield, S. D., *Understanding and Facilitating Adult Learning.* Milton Keynes, Open University Press, 1986.

Brookfield, S. D. and Preskill, S., *Discussion as a Way of Teaching.* Buckingham, Open University Press, 1999.

Brown, A., *Groupwork.* 3rd edition. Aldershot, Ashgate, 1994.

Brown, R., *Group Processes: Dynamics Within and Between Groups.* Oxford, Blackwell, 1988.

Burridge, R. A., *John.* Oxford, Bible Reading Fellowship, 1998.

Burrows, D., Mind the Gap – a Reflection on a Franciscan Understanding of Collaborative Ministry. <www.orders.anglican.org/tssf/fstudies/ Franciscan%20Collaborative%20Ministry.pdf>, 2005, accessed 8 October 2007.

Buzan, T., *The Ultimate Book of Mind Maps.* London, HarperCollins, 2005.

Callahan, S., Rixon, A. and Shenk, M., *The Ultimate Guide to Anecdote Circles*, 2006. <http://www.anecdote.com.au/files/Ultimate_Guide_to_ACs_v1.0.pdf>, accessed 17 January 2008.

Carlson, R., *Don't Sweat the Small Stuff*. London, Hodder & Stoughton, 1997.

Carter, W. J., *Team Spirituality*. Nashville, Abingdon, 1997.

Charities Evaluation Services, *What is Evaluation?* Undated. <http://www.ces-vol.org.uk/index.cfm?pg=167> accessed 28 January 2008.

Charities Evaluation Services, *What to Include in an Evaluation brief*, 2004. <http://www.ces-vol.org.uk/index.cfm?format=16>, accessed 28 January 2008.

Christou, S., *Evangelism and Collaborative Ministry*. Eastbourne, Phoenix Books, 2004.

Church of England, *Training for Collaboration in Ministry: Promoting Good Practice in IME*. Archbishops' Council. London, Church House, 2003.

Clark, D., Reclaiming vocation for the whole people of God. In *Management and Ministry*, J. Nelson, ed. Norwich, Canterbury Press, 1996.

Conroy, M., *Looking into the Well*. Chicago, Loyola University Press, 1995.

Cormack, D., *Change Directions*. Crowborough, Monarch, 1995.

Covey, S., *The Seven Habits of Highly Effective People*. London, Simon & Schuster UK, 1989.

De Bary, E., *Theological Reflection*. Collegeville, Liturgical Press, 2003.

De Bono, E., *Six Thinking Hats*, 2nd edition. London, Penguin, 2000.

Del Tufo, S., *What is Evaluation?* 2002. <http://www.evaluationtrust.org/evaluation>, accessed 28 January 2008.

Edmondson, C., *Fit to Lead*. London, Darton, Longman & Todd, 2002.

Estés, C. P., *Women Who Run with the Wolves*. London, Rider, 1992.

Evaluation Trust, *Toolkit*, undated. <http://www.evaluationtrust.org/tools/toolkit>, accessed 28 January 2008.

Farley, E., Ecclesial contextual thinking. In *Shaping a Theological Mind*, D. C. Marks, ed. Aldershot, Ashgate, 2002.

Fisher, S., Ibrahim, A. D., Ludin, J., Smith, R., Williams, S. and Williams, S., *Working with Conflict: Skills and Strategies for Action*. Birmingham, Zed Books and Responding to Conflict, 2000.

Fitchett, G., *Assessing Spiritual Need*. Lima OH, Academic Renewal Press, 2002.

Foster, R., *Celebration of Discipline*. London, Hodder & Stoughton, 1980.

Freeth, D., Sustaining interprofessional collaboration. *Journal of Interprofessional Care* 15(1):37–46, 2001.

Goffee, R. and Jones, G., *Why Should Anyone Be Led by You?* Boston, Harvard Business School Press, 2006.

Greenleaf, R. K., *Servant Leadership*. Mahwah, Paulist Press, 1977.

Greenwood, R., *The Ministry Team Handbook*. London, SPCK, 2000.

Greenwood, R., *Transforming Church*. London, SPCK, 2002.

Grundy, M., *Understanding Congregations*. London, Geoffrey Chapman, 1998.

Bibliography

Grundy, M., *What's New in Church Leadership?* London, Canterbury Press, 2007.

Handy, C., *Understanding Organizations.* 4th edition. London, Penguin, 1993.

Harris, V., ed., *Community Work Skills Manual.* Newcastle, Association of Community Workers, 2001.

Hawkins, P. and Shohet, R., *Supervision in the Helping Professions*, 2nd edition. Buckingham, Open University Press, 2000.

Honey, P. and Mumford, A., *The Manual of Learning Styles.* Maidenhead, Peter Honey, 1992.

Hooker, R. and Sargant, J., *Belonging to Britain: Christian Perspectives on a Plural Society.* London, CCBI, undated.

Hudson, J., *Evaluating Ministry.* Herndon, Alban Institute, 1998.

Ingram, G. and Harris, J., *Delivering Good Youth Work.* Lyme Regis, Russell House, 2001.

Janis, I. L., *Victims of Groupthink.* Boston, Houghton Mifflin Company, 1972.

Jaques, D., *Learning in Groups.* London, Kogan Page, 1992.

Johns, C., *Becoming a Reflective Practitioner*, 2nd edition. Oxford, Blackwell, 2004.

Katzenbach, J. R. and Smith, D. K., *The Wisdom of Teams: Creating the High-Performance Organisation.* London, McGraw-Hill, 1996.

Killen, P. O. and de Beer, J., *The Art of Theological Reflection.* New York, Crossroad, 1999.

Kinast, R. L., *Let Ministry Teach.* Collegeville, Liturgical Press, 1996.

Lahad, M., *Creative Supervision.* London, Jessica Kingsley, 2000.

Lank, E., *Collaborative Advantage.* Basingstoke, Palgrave Macmillan, 2006.

Lovell, G., *Consultancy, Ministry and Mission.* London, Burns and Oates, 2000.

Macbeth, F. and Fine, N., *Playing with Fire: Creative Conflict Resolution for Young Adults.* Gabriola Island, New Society Publishers, 1995.

Macchia, S. A., *Becoming a Healthy Team.* Grand Rapids, Baker Books, 2005.

McDonald, I., *Collaborative Youth Work within South Middlesborough.* Centre for Youth Ministry. Unpublished dissertation, 2007.

Mackinnon, J., Academic supervision: seeking metaphors and models for quality. *Journal of Further and Higher Education*, 28(4): 395–405, 2004.

Mallison, J., *The Small Group Leader: A Manual to Develop Vital Small Groups.* Bletchley, Scripture Union, 1996.

Malphurs, A., *Developing a Vision for Ministry.* 2nd edition. Grand Rapids, Baker Books, 1999.

Manor, O., *Choosing a Groupwork Approach: An Inclusive Stance.* London, Jessica Kingsley, 2000.

Marshall, E. W., *Transforming the Way We Work.* New York, American Management Association, 1995.

Middleton, J., *Beyond Authority.* Basingstoke, Palgrave, 2007.

Bibliography

Moon, J. A., *Reflection in Learning and Professional Development*. London, Kogan Page, 2000.

Morrison, T., *Staff Supervision in Social Care*. Brighton, Pavilion Publishing, 1996.

Nelson, J., ed. *Management and Ministry*. Norwich, Canterbury Press, 1996.

O'Sullivan, R., *Practicing Evaluation: A Collaborative Approach*. Thousand Oaks, Sage, 2004.

Owen, H., Hodgson, V. and Gazzard, N., *The Leadership Manual*. Harlow, Pearson Prentice Hall Business, 2004.

Payne, M., *Teamwork in Multiprofessional Care*. Basingstoke, Macmillan, 2000.

Pearman, R. G., *I'm Not Crazy, I'm Just Not You*. Mountain View, Davies Black Publishing, 1998.

Pearson, G., Designing a learning covenant. In *Experiencing Ministry Supervision*, W. T. Pyle and M. A. Seal, eds. Nashville, Broadman & Holman, 1995.

Perkins, D., *King Arthur's Round Table*. Hoboken, Wiley, 2003.

Pimlott, J., Pimlott, N. and Wiles, D., *Inspire Too! More Fresh Ideas for Creative Youth Work*. Birmingham, Frontier Youth Trust, 2005.

Pimlott, N., *Evaluation: An Uninvited Guest*. Birmingham, Frontier Youth Trust, 2008.

Pohly, K., *Transforming the Rough Places: The Ministry of Supervision*. Dayton, Whaleprints, 1993.

Pyle, W. T. and Seals, M. A., eds. *Experiencing Ministry Supervision*. Nashville, Broadman and Holman, 1995.

Quenk, N., *Was That Really Me? How Everyday Stress Brings out Our Hidden Personality*, revised edition. Mountain View, Davies Black Publishing, 2002.

Riddell, M., *alt.spirit@metro.m3*. Oxford, Lion, 1997.

Ringer, T. M., *Group Action: The Dynamics of Groups in Therapeutic, Educational and Corporate Settings*. London, Jessica Kingsley, 2002.

Rixon, A., *The 5 Advantages of Using Story in Evaluation*, 2006. <http://www.zahmoo.com/blog/index.php?p=13&more=1&c=1>, accessed 17 January 2008.

Robertson, D., *Collaborative Ministry*. Oxford, Bible Reading Fellowship, 2007.

Rogers, J., *Adults Learning*. Milton Keynes, Open University Press, 1971.

Rupp, J., *Dear Heart, Come Home*. New York, Crossroad, 1996.

Sawyer, K., *Group Genius: The Creative Power of Collaboration*. Cambridge, Basic Books, 2007.

Schon, D. A., *The Reflective Practitioner*. Aldershot, Ashgate, 1991.

Senge, P., *The Fifth Discipline: The Art and Practice of the Learning Organisation*, revised edition. London, Random House, 2006.

Shaw, I. F., Greene, J. C. and Mark, M. M., *The Sage Handbook of Evaluation*. London, Sage, 2006.

Shaw, P., *Mirroring Jesus as Leader*. Cambridge, Grove Books, 2004.

Sheppard, D. and Warlock, D., *Better Together*. London, Hodder & Stoughton, 1988.

Sofield, L. and Juliano, C., *Collaborative Ministry*. Notre Dame, Ave Maria Press, 1987.

Squirrell, G., *Becoming an Effective Trainer*. Lyme Regis, Russell House, 1998.

Stevens, P., The supervisory conference. In *Experiencing Ministry Supervision*, W. T. Pyle and M. A. Seals, eds. Nashville, Broadman & Holman, 1995.

Stibbe, M., *John*. Sheffield, JSOT Press, 1993.

Subhra, G., *Reclaiming the Evaluation Agenda*. Derby, University of Derby, 2004.

Tanner, K., How I changed my mind. In *Shaping a Theological Mind*, D. C. Marks, ed. Aldershot, Ashgate, 2002.

Thompson, N., *People Problems: A Toolkit of Techniques*. London, Kogan Page, 2006.

Thompson, N., *People Skills*. London, Macmillan, 1996.

Thompson, N., *Promoting Equality*. Basingstoke, Macmillan, 1998.

Tidball, D., *Builders and Fools*. Leicester, IVP, 1999.

Van der Ven, J. A., *Education for Reflective Ministry*. Louvain, Peeters Press, 1998.

Vine, W. E., *An Expository Dictionary of New Testament Words*. Chicago, Moody Press, 1985.

vision *n.*, *The New Oxford American Dictionary*, 2nd edition. Oxford University Press, 2005. *Oxford Reference Online*. Oxford University Press. Oxford Brookes University, accessed 15 October 2007. <http://www.oxfordreference.com/views/ENTRY.html?subview=Main&entry=t183.e85229>.

Weisbord, M. R., *Discovering Common Ground*. San Francisco, Berrett-Koehler, 1992.

Whitehead, E. E. and Whitehead, J. D., *The Promise of Partnership*. Lincoln, Backinprint.com, 1991.

Whitney, D. and Trosten-Bloom, A., *The Power of Appreciative Inquiry*. San Francisco, Berrett-Koehler, 2003.

Further reading

1   Introduction to collaborative ministry

Adair, J., *Leadership Skills*. London, Institute of Personnel Development, 1997.
Classic – all his books are helpful, he is a Christian who writes predominantly for the business field.

Greenleaf, R. K., *Servant Leadership*. Mahwah, Paulist Press, 1977.
Classic on servant leadership.

Grundy, M., *What's New in Church Leadership?* London, Canterbury Press, 2007.
Recent thinking from a church perspective includes collaborative ministry.

Robertson, D., *Collaborative Ministry*. Oxford, The Bible Reading Fellowship, 2007.
Has a strong biblical basis for collaborative ministry and written for UK context.

Whitehead, E. E. and Whitehead, J. D., *The Promise of Partnership*. Lincoln, Backinprint.com, 1991.
Insightful and good on psychological perspectives.

2   Groupwork processes for collaborative ministry

Jaques, D., *Learning in Groups*. London, Kogan Page, 1992.
Although set in a learning context, contains principles, models and reflections relevant to broader groupwork practice.

Mallison, J., *The Small Group Leader: A Manual to Develop Vital Small Groups*. Bletchley, Scripture Union, 1996.
Good sourcebook regarding leading groups in a Christian context.

Neri, C., *Group*. London, Jessica Kingsley Publishers, 1998.
Helpful exploration of psychodynamic processes in groups.

Ringer, T. M., *Group Action: The Dynamics of Groups in Therapeutic, Educational and Corporate Settings*. London, Jessica Kingsley Publishers, 2002.
Useful exploration of psychodynamic processes in groups.

3   Facilitation skills

Chambers, R., *Participatory Workshops: A Sourcebook of 21 Sets of Ideas and Activities*. London, Earthscan Publications, 2002.

Useful small book with a range of practical ideas for facilitating groups.

Darley, S. and Heath, W., *The Expressive Arts Activity Book*. London, Jessica Kingsley, 2008.

Ideas book written for therapeutic contexts but the ideas translate well to other areas of groupwork.

Hogan, C., *Facilitation Skills: A Toolkit of Techniques*. London, Kogan Page, 2005.

More in-depth exploration of facilitation skills.

Schwarz, R., *The Skilled Facilitator*. 2nd edition. San Francisco, Jossey-Bass, 2002.

Another in-depth exploration of facilitation skills.

Shepard, C. and Treseder, P., *Participation: Spice It Up*. Cardiff, Save the Children Fund, 2002.

Helpful and creative approaches to encouraging participation.

Silberman, M., *101 Ways to Make Training Active*. San Francisco, Jossey-Bass/Pfeiffer, 1995.

Practical activities for training and other group contexts.

4 Reflecting skills

Ballard, P. and Pritchard, J., *Practical Theology in Action*, 2nd edition. London, SPCK, 2006.

A range of methods of doing theology.

Johns, C., *Becoming a Reflective Practitioner*. 2nd edition. Oxford, Blackwell, 2004.

Good introduction but written for the healthcare field.

Killen, P. O. and De Beer, J., *The Art of Theological Reflection*. New York, Crossroad, 1999.

Comprehensive text.

Moon, J. A., *Reflection in Learning and Professional Development*. London, Kogan Page, 2000.

Excellent introduction to the topic.

Nash, P., *What Theology for Youth Work?* Cambridge, Grove Books, 2007.

Explores four different approaches to doing theology.

5 Vision-building skills

Cormack, D., *Change Directions*. Crowborough, Monarch, 1995.

Helpful step-by-step approach.

Lovell, G., *Consultancy, Ministry and Mission*. London, Burns & Oates, 2000.

Lots of useful ideas if you are asked to help facilitate a vision building process.

Malphurs, A., *Developing a Vision for Ministry*. 2nd edition. Grand Rapids, Baker Books, 1999.
Biblically based approach.

6   Teamwork skills

Adair, J., *Effective Teambuilding*. London, Gower, 1986.
Practical exploration of ideas and principles around teamwork.
Belbin, R. M., *Management Teams: Why They Succeed or Fail*. Oxford, Butterworth–Heinemann, 1981.
More in-depth exploration of team role theory.
Belbin, R. M., *Team Roles at Work*. Oxford, Butterworth–Heinemann, 1993.
Explores team role theory in greater depth.
Katzenbach, J. R. and Smith, D. K., *The Wisdom of Teams: Creating the High-Performance Organisation*. London, McGraw-Hill, 1996.
Exploration of principles and practical approaches to building teams.
Miller, B. C., *Quick Team-building Activities for Busy Managers*. New York, Amacom, 2003.
Suggestions of practical activities to use in team-building.
Newstrom, J. and Scannell, E. E., *The Big Book of Teambuilding Games*. San Francisco, Jossey-Bass, 1997.
Practical games and activities.

7   Supervision skills

Hawkins, P. and Shohet, R., *Supervision in the Helping Professions*. 2nd edition. Buckingham, Open University Press, 2000.
Comprehensive and sophisticated in approach.
Herbert, M. and Nash, S., *Supervising Youth Workers*. Cambridge, Grove P105, 2006.
Explores the minister–youth worker dynamic in supervision.
Lahad, M., *Creative Supervision*. London, Jessica Kingsley Publisher, 2000.
Lots of ideas that help you do supervision differently.
Lamdin, K. and Tilley, D., *Supporting New Ministers in the Local Church*. London, SPCK, 2007.
Detailed and accessible book for those managing other ministers with relevant material for any ministry staff context.
Morrison, T., *Staff Supervision in Social Care*. Brighton, Pavilion Publishing, 1996.
Good material on games playing.
Thompson, N., *People Problems*. Basingstoke, Palgrave, 2006.
Lots of practical ideas to help deal with people problems.

8 Conflict skills

Macbeth, F. and Fine, N., *Playing with Fire: Creative Conflict Resolution for Young Adults*. Gabriola Island, New Society Publishers, 1995.
Practical resources for exploring conflict, designed for work with young adults but could be used in any context.
Stubbs, D. R., *Assertiveness at Work*. London, Pan Books, 1997.
Practical assertiveness skills.
Thompson, N., *People Problems: A Toolkit of Techniques*. London, Kogan Page, 2006.
A highly practical book with suggestions of 50 different approaches to conflict.
Thompson, N., *People Skills*. London, Macmillan, 1996.
Explores a range of different skills which are helpful in work with people, many of these have relevance to conflict situations.

Mediation at Work <www.mediationatwork.com>.

9 Diversity skills

Quenk, N., *Was That Really Me? How Everyday Stress Brings out Our Hidden Personality* (revised edition). Mountain View, Davies Black Publishing, 2002.
Help with self-awareness and dealing with others.
Thompson, N., *People Problems: A Toolkit of Techniques*. London, Kogan Page, 2006.
Practical ideas.
Thompson, N., *Promoting Equality*. Basingstoke, Macmillan, 1998.
Helpful for understanding wider perspectives.

10 Evaluation skills

Bryman, A., *Social Research Methods*. Oxford, Oxford University Press, 2001.
Good overview of qualitative research methods.
O'Sullivan, R., *Practicing Evaluation*. Thousand Oaks, Sage, 2004.
A book about doing evaluation collaboratively.
Shaw, I. F., Greene, J. C. and Mark, M. M., *The Sage Handbook of Evaluation*. London, Sage, 2006.
One of the most comprehensive books on the topic.
Subhra, G., *Reclaiming the Evaluation Agenda*. Derby, University of Derby, 2004.
Lots of accessible approaches to evaluation.

This is an area where there are a range of good quality websites which provide most of the information you need to complete a basic evaluation. See, for example:

Charities Evaluation Services <www.ces-vol.org.uk>. PQASSO is an accessible package designed for the voluntary sector which is recommended if you want to undertake a comprehensive evaluation and don't know where to begin. It is available through Charities Evaluation Services.

Evaluation Trust <www.evaluation.trust.org>

W. K. Kellogg Foundation <www.wkkf.org>

Index

Index

qualities of collaborative workers
9–10

reflecting skills 47–62; issues 56–8;
layers of reflection 49; problem-
solving 59–60; processes 50–4;
reflecting in groups 58–9;
theological perspectives 60–1;
tools 50–2
reflective practice 48–50
roles 26–7

Schon, Donald 54
self-awareness 33–4
Senge, Peter 63, 111
SMART objectives 67, 70, 74
supervision 92–107; contracts and
covenants 97–9; definition 94–5;
functions of supervisor 96; group
supervision 101; issues and
problems 102–3; making
supervision work 103–4;

metaphors 100; models 99–100;
responsibilities 96–7; theological
perspectives 101–2; tools for
supervision 104–7

teamwork 77–91; aims 81–2;
growing teams 86–7; hazards
89–90; identity 80–1; leadership
82; roles 83–6; theological
perspectives 79–80
theological reflection 52–3
Thompson, Neil 33, 48, 50, 108, 121,
126, 154
Trinity 4–5
Tuckman, Bruce 18–23

vision-building 63–76;
communicating vision 67;
definition 67–8; theological
perspectives 65–7; tools 68–75

wisdom 44–5, 60

Also available in the
SPCK Library of Ministry series

COMMUNITY AND MINISTRY
An Introduction to Community Development
in a Christian Context

Paul Ballard and Lesley Husselbee

All clergy, ministers, church-related community workers and lay leaders need to understand how they and their churches may relate to the community in which they are set. This book provides a thorough and professional introduction to the subject, and includes discussion about:

- what community is
- community work and mission
- models of community work
- ethnic, cultural and religious diversity
- the local authority and voluntary agencies
- working with volunteers
- spirituality in community participation

'This book aims to take on the challenge of equipping people with the skills, understanding and information to critically explore the field of community and ministry. It is a timely publication given the increasing government acknowledgement of the contribution of faith communities in both urban and rural community development and regeneration.'

Jim Robertson, Chair of Enabling Group,
Churches' Community Work Alliance

Paul Ballard is Emeritus Professor in the School of Religious and Theological Studies, Cardiff University, where he taught Practical Theology. He has had active involvement in community development, as a consultant with church-based projects, and as a member of the Community Resource Unit of the British Council of Churches. With John Pritchard he has written *Practical Theology in Action* (SPCK, new edition 2006).

Lesley Husselbee is Tutor in Church and Community Education at Northern College, Manchester (which forms part of Luther King House College). She was Secretary for Training in the United Reformed Church (URC) and has also been Senior Lecturer in Urban Geography at the Roehampton Institute, London. She has published with the National Christian Education Council and Roots (an educational resource supported by Churches Together in Britain and Ireland).

ISBN: 978–0–281–05800–6

SUPPORTING NEW MINISTERS IN THE LOCAL CHURCH

A Handbook

Keith Lamdin and David Tilley

This book is designed to help those who supervise new ministers at the start of their ordained ministry. It will also be relevant and useful to all people taking up new appointments: the ministers themselves, ordinands on placement, youth ministers and pastoral assistants, preachers, Readers and lay ministers in all denominations.

It offers:

- ideas for good practice
- possibilities for solving problems
- different models of adult learning and supervision
- practical ways of working together with a curate

Professional supervision and mentoring is widely used in other professions, such as medicine, nursing, social work and legal practice. The Church also needs professional competence and has much to learn, as well as to share, in this area.

'This book offers both wisdom and the fruit of practical experience in the area of supervision of colleagues in ministry and will be a useful aid to those – incumbent or curate – embarking on this significant ministry.'

The Ven. Christopher Lowson,
Director of Ministry, Archbishops' Council

Keith Lamdin is Director of Stewardship, Training, Evangelism and Ministry in the Diocese of Oxford.

David Tilley has worked in the training of Methodist ministers and in Continuing Ministerial Education of clergy in the Coventry Diocese.

ISBN: 978–0–281–05879–2

Also available from SPCK in the
New Library of Pastoral Care

THE PASTORAL CARE OF PEOPLE
WITH MENTAL HEALTH PROBLEMS

Marion L. S. Carson

As a minister or pastoral worker, it is highly likely that at some stage in your ministry you will find yourself caring for people with psychiatric problems and their families. *The Pastoral Care of People with Mental Health Problems* is an invaluable resource to help you provide support for those suffering from the most common problems, such as depression, Alzheimer's disease, anorexia, addiction to drugs or alcohol, post-traumatic stress disorder, bipolar disorder, schizophrenia and anti-social personality disorder.

As well as outlining the main psychiatric conditions and their treatments, the book examines the particular issues facing pastoral workers and discusses some of the ethical issues involved. Using a wealth of illustrations, it offers practical advice and guidance for the care of individuals and families who find their lives turned upside down by psychiatric illness, addressing questions such as:

- How can I help the family of a young girl who cuts herself?
- What is the difference between depression and an abnormal grief reaction?
- How can I distinguish between a symptom of mental illness and genuine religious revelation?

In cases of severe mental illness it will be necessary to work alongside medical, nursing and social work staff, and guidance is given on how best to do this.

The Pastoral Care of People with Mental Health Problems is the fruit of Marion Carson's many years of experience as a practising psychiatric nurse, her teaching in a theological college and her involvement in pastoral care provision in a local church setting.

ISBN: 978–0–281–05866–2

Also available from SPCK in the
New Library of Pastoral Care

ALL GOD'S CHILDREN
An Introduction to Pastoral Work with Children

This helpful and practical book offers theological, sociological and psychological insights on childhood and the care and nurture of children within the Church. Marian Carter also includes questions to stimulate personal reflection and to encourage discussion and interaction in groups.

'This book shows the complexity and richness of the interplay between who children are (and how they can also teach us adults about our own spiritual maturity) and their pastoral care by adults. It should be read slowly and mindfully, but it can also be used as a handy reference for orientation in this rapidly growing and changing field.'

Jerome W. Berryman, Executive Director
The Center for the Theology of Childhood, Houston, Texas

'Marian Carter's *All God's Children* is a brilliant book. There are many books about how children develop. Advice abounds on how children should be brought up. There are plenty of handbooks to guide Sunday school teachers and clergy in their ministry to children. But there are very few serious studies of what, as Christians, we are to believe about children and of how childhood is to be understood from the perspective of Christian faith. Marian Carter's extraordinary achievement – and I know of no other book that has quite done this – is to ground an eminently practical discussion of how children should be nurtured, whether at home or in church, on a firm theological foundation. This is "applied theology" at its very best.'

John Pridmore, Vicar of St-John-at-Hackney
Committee member, Church of England's Strategy for Children

Marian Carter is a priest and a former teacher in primary and secondary education. She trained teachers and taught pastoral theology on the South West Ministerial Training Course and at the University College of St Mark and St John. She has written several publications on all-age learning and worship.

ISBN: 978–0–281–05888–4